brunch

brunch

Brilliant ideas for successful entertaining

Rachel Lee

McRae Books

Publishers: Anne McRae, Marco Nardi
Project Director: Anne McRae
Design Directors: Marco Nardi, Sara Mathews
Text: Rachel Lee
Photography: David Munns
Food Styling: Tonia George, Vicky Musselman
Styling: Victoria Munns
Layouts: Adina Stefania Dragomir
Editing: Helen Farrell
Colour separations: Fotolito Toscana
Printed in Italy

ISBN: 88-89272-66-X
This book was conceived, edited and designed by
McRae Books Srl
Borgo Santa Croce, 8 - 50122 Florence, Italy
info@mcraebooks.com

Contents

Brunch: cooking, eating, and relaxing with friends

Sunday brunch has always been my favorite meal. It is the time of the week that we can allow ourselves to slow down and really enjoy a meal. There is nowhere we have to be, no rush—so why not have another glass of champagne? It is a meal completely in the moment, relaxed, surrounded by good food and happy company.

My first job at 14 was working Sunday brunch at a seaside California restaurant. I remember lots of laughter as customers basked in the sunny garden sipping mimosas. Sunday brunch was also the busiest shift of the week, and at times the abundance of cheap sparkling wine seemed to compensate for the quality of food coming out of the kitchen. Brunch in a restaurant can be jolly, but unless you have a tried and true favorite café, it can be crowded and loud, and the "special" can taste like something reinvented from the Saturday night leftovers. At a certain point I started hosting brunch parties at home because it seemed like the nicest, most relaxed way to spend a Sunday with friends. We could eat and laugh for hours without worrying about finding a table in a busy restaurant or overstaying our welcome with a waiter wanting to give our table to another group.

I cook because I love to eat, and I believe cooking should be fun, an enjoyable extension of eating. I tell my cooking class students to grab a glass of wine because we all cook better when we are relaxed and not afraid to try something new. If you are not having fun in the kitchen, the meal will not be as good. Especially in the case of brunch, the cook should be having as much fun as the guests, not slaving over the stove or stressed about putting on a big spread.

For this reason, I have tried to create brunch menus for which most of the items can be prepared in advance. The idea is that the cook wants to have an enjoyable weekend cooking and eating with friends. The shopping and most of the cooking can be done on a Saturday, with only a few items to finish on Sunday morning before the brunch. So, no leaping up at the crack of dawn.

Also, do not feel you have to make all the dishes on each brunch menu. Some of the menus are large and ambitious, for when you really have the itch to cook up a storm. But in general, the menus are more useful as a list of possible dishes to serve. Make only what you want. Mix and match. The only rule is to have a good time.

The menus have themes to give them a sense of cohesion, but they are not meant to be "authentic." If you are Mexican or English or Italian, these are not the recipes your mother made when you were growing up. All the recipes are my own interpretation, and I have taken loads of creative license. You should too. Cooking is a creative process. If you don't have an ingredient, improvise. Be adventurous, follow your nose. We have become so wrapped up in a celebrity cooking culture that we are often too intimidated to trust our own senses. You are the expert about what tastes good. Some of my favorite recipes grew out of "mistakes."

The main guideline I follow (which makes it difficult to produce a bad meal) is cooking with fresh, seasonal ingredients whenever possible. The better the ingredients, the better the dish. Tomatoes need to taste of tomatoes, and they are not going to taste of anything if they are picked green in a foreign country, shipped thousands of miles, and then gassed to turn red. Wait for produce to be in season and buy from local farmers if you can. The same is true for animal and dairy products. Local, free-range, and organic meat and dairy products taste better, I believe, because the animal has had a happier, healthier life and there are no preservatives and antibiotics to interfere with the flavor. This does not have to be a militant, political issue; for me it is more common sense and a desire to eat well.

But above all, invite over a few of your closest friends, open a bottle of sparkling wine, and play in the kitchen. And may the process be as pleasurable as the outcome.

November in Tuscany

Crostini Neri
Bruschette with New Olive Oil and Cavolo Nero
Squash, Chestnut, and Ginger Soup
Quail with Fresh Herbs, Chanterelles, and Polenta
Fennel, Radicchio, and Orange Salad
Walnut-Leaf Pecorino with Corbezzolo Honey
Poached Quince Meringue Pie

Wine Suggestions:
Rosso di Montalcino (Piancornello, Siro Pacenti,
or Fattoi), Moscadello di Montalcino (Caprili)

November, when the first olives are pressed, is one of my favorite times to cook in Tuscany. Nothing beats a simple bruschetta: a slice of toasted peasant-style bread, with a rub of garlic, a pinch of sea salt, and a generous pour of newly cold-pressed extra-virgin olive oil. It is a supreme delight, and explains why Tuscan cooking is so popular. Tuscany does not offer complex cuisine; it just has the best ingredients put together simply so that none of the flavors are lost.

November is also when the woods are bursting with wild mushrooms, the first of the white winter truffles are found, and dark leafy greens, cabbages, and root vegetables are piled high in the farmers' markets. My neighbor's orchard is full of golden pears, fragrant quince, and crunchy apples. Hunters are bringing home pheasants, quail, hare, and wild boar for the dinner table. Nature is in its last throes of production before the first frosts.

Crostini Neri (Chicken Liver Toasts)

8 oz (250 g) chicken livers and hearts

2 tablespoons extra-virgin olive oil

1 medium red onion, chopped

A pinch of red pepper flakes

1 bay leaf

1 salted anchovy, filleted, or 3 anchovy fillets under oil

2 cloves garlic, minced

2 tablespoons finely chopped fresh Italian flat-leaf parsley

1/2 teaspoon minced fresh thyme

2 tablespoons Cognac or brandy

4 tablespoons dry white wine

2 tablespoon unsalted butter

1 tablespoon finely grated lemon zest

3 tablespoons finely grated parmesan

2 tablespoons salted capers, rinsed and soaked
    for 15 minutes, drained and finely chopped

Salt and freshly ground black pepper to taste

1 red onion, sliced paper thin, for garnish

1/2 lemon

30 Italian parsley leaves, finely chopped, for garnish

1 baguette (French loaf), cut into thin medallion slices

PLANNING AHEAD: This pâté is even better the day after it is made since the flavors have had time to meld. Rinse the chicken livers and hearts. Cut away any green areas and tough, fatty membranes. Chop the hearts and livers and set aside.

Heat the olive oil in a medium skillet (frying pan) over medium heat. Add the onion and red pepper flakes and sauté gently until the onion is soft. Add the chicken livers and hearts, bay leaf, anchovy, garlic, parsley, and thyme. Slowly brown the livers, scraping the sides of the pan with a wooden spoon to collect all the onions and juices that will become thick and almost caramelized. When the livers are browned, add the Cognac and cook until it has evaporated. Pour in the wine and let reduce until the pan sauces become thick and syrupy again. Remove from the heat. Stir in the butter. Cool to room temperature.

Remove the bay leaf. Put the liver mixture into a food processor (scrape the pan with a spatula to get all the juices) and pulse to a fairly smooth paste. Leave some texture, but no large chunks. Transfer the liver mixture to a large bowl. Stir in the parmesan, lemon zest, and capers. Mix well. Taste for salt and pepper. Cover and refrigerate until ready to use.

Squeeze the half lemon over the thin slices of red onion and sprinkle with salt. Marinate for 10 minutes. When ready to serve, toast the bread (on a baking sheet in the oven if making lots of crostini). Spread the warm toast with a layer of the pâté. Garnish with the slices of marinated red onion and the chopped parsley.

Bruschette with New Olive Oil and Cavolo Nero

2 lb (1 kg) cavolo nero or kale

Loaf of good quality Tuscan-style bread, cut into 1/2-inch
    (1-cm) slices

1 clove garlic, peeled

1 cup (250 ml) newly cold pressed, extra-virgin olive oil

Coarse sea salt to taste

Salt and freshly ground black pepper to taste

Tuscans are known for their love of dark, leafy greens. *Cavolo nero*, or kale, appears in the farmers' markets about the same time as the new oil emerges from the olive mills, and together they make a healthy and delicious fall treat. I like to make a platter of plain bruschette and a platter with the cavolo nero.

Bring 1 quart (1 liter) of water to a boil in a 6-quart (6-liter) stainless steel pot. Wash the kale and discard the tough stalks. Slice each leaf down the middle of its central membrane, then coarsely chop. Sprinkle some coarse sea salt into the boiling water and drop in the kale. When the water returns to boil, reduce the heat to a simmer, and partially cover the pot. Simmer the kale until tender, approximately 30 minutes. Drain in a colander.

Toast the bread. Lightly rub the garlic across the toasted bread and place the slices on a large serving platter or individual plates. Top each slice with a mound of the kale. Pour the olive oil over the kale (be generous with the oil). Salt to taste. Sprinkle with pepper, if desired. Serve warm.

Crostini Neri and Bruschette with New Olive Oil and Cavolo Nero

Squash, Chestnut, and Ginger Soup

1 lb (500 g) fresh chestnuts

1 tablespoon butter

2 tablespoons extra-virgin olive oil

1 medium yellow onion, chopped

1 carrot, peeled and chopped

1 celery stalk, chopped

1/8 teaspoon red pepper flakes

3 cloves garlic, minced

2 tablespoons minced fresh ginger

1¾ lb (800 g) butternut squash, peeled
    and cut into 1 inch (2.5 cm) cubes

12 oz (350 g) sweet potatoes, peeled
    and cut into 1 inch (2.5 cm) cubes

2 medium Yukon Gold potatoes, peeled
    and cut into 1 inch (2.5 cm) cubes

1 teaspoon coarse sea salt

1 quart (1 liter) Quick Stock (see page 138)

Salt and freshly ground black pepper to taste

Extra-virgin olive oil and fresh chives, to garnish

The sweet nuttiness of the squash and chestnuts marry beautifully with the spiciness of the ginger. This is rich, creamy soup without the calories of cream.

PLANNING AHEAD: This soup is excellent the next day. The chestnuts can be roasted and the stock can be made in advance.

Roast the chestnuts over the fire, or with a sharp knife cut an x on the shell of each chestnut, place on a baking sheet and toast in a preheated 400°F/200°C/gas 6 oven until they split open (about 15 minutes). Allow to cool.

Peel and chop the chestnuts. You will need 1 cup (250 g) of chopped chestnuts for the soup.

In a 3-quart (3-liter) heavy saucepan over medium heat, melt the butter with the olive oil. Add the onion, carrot, celery, and red pepper flakes. Sauté slowly until the onion is soft but not brown. Add the garlic, ginger, squash, sweet potatoes, potatoes, sea salt, chopped chestnuts, and stock. There should be enough stock to cover all the vegetables and for the vegetables to move about easily when stirred. If not, add more stock or water. Bring to a boil, then cover and simmer on lowest heat for 1 hour, stirring occasionally. Add more stock or water if the soup appears dry or begins to stick to the bottom of the pan. The squash and potatoes should fall apart when pierced with a fork.

Purée the soup in batches in a blender (use caution when blending hot liquids and be sure the blender has a well-fitting lid). Taste for salt and pepper.

Serve with a drizzle of your best extra-virgin olive oil and sprinkle with the chopped chives.

Quail with Fresh Herbs, Chanterelles, and Polenta

6 whole quail

3 tablespoons extra-virgin olive oil

1/2 cup (60 g) pancetta, chopped

1/2 cup (80 g) diced shallots

5 fresh sage leaves

1/2 teaspoon salt

1 teaspoon freshly ground black pepper

1 bay leaf

4 large cloves garlic, thinly sliced

4 tablespoons minced Italian flat-leaf parsley

3 tablespoons minced fresh thyme

2 tablespoons minced fresh marjoram

1 teaspoon finely grated lemon zest

3 tablespoons grappa or brandy

4 tablespoons dry white wine

4 tablespoons Quick Stock (see page 138) or water

2 tablespoons unsalted butter

3 cups (750 ml) coarsely chopped fresh chanterelles
   (cleaned with paper towels and as little water as possible)

PLANNING AHEAD: Start cooking the polenta (see page 139) 1^1/$_2$ hours before beginning the quail so that it is creamy and ready to serve by the time the quail are finished. The cooked quail can be kept warm, covered in the pan, for 30 minutes before serving.

Clean the quail of any stray feathers and trim away any dark skin around the necks and rear cavities. Rinse and pat dry thoroughly with paper towels. Tie the legs of each quail together with a small piece of butcher's string.

Heat the olive oil in a 12-inch (30-cm) skillet (frying pan) over medium heat. Add the quail, turning them gently with two wooden spoons, until they are thoroughly browned on all sides. Use a splatter screen if the hot oil is spitting. When the quail are deep brown, carefully pour off the fat in the pan. Return the quail to medium heat. Add the pancetta. After 2 minutes add the shallots and sage. Season the birds with the salt and pepper. When the shallots are soft and translucent and the pancetta is cooked, add the bay leaf, garlic, parsley, thyme, marjoram, lemon zest, and grappa. Give the grappa 1 minute to evaporate, then stir in the wine. Cook uncovered for 3–5 minutes, scraping the glaze from the bottom and sides of the pan. Pour in the stock or water, cover the pan with a lid, reduce heat to low, and simmer for 10 minutes. Check to make sure there is enough liquid in the pan and that the shallots and herbs are not getting scorched. Add a little more stock or water if the pan is dry. Cover and continue cooking for another 5–10 minutes. The quail are done when the legs move easily in their sockets.

Remove the cooked quail from the pan and place on a warm serving platter in the oven while you finish the sauce. Cut and remove the butcher's string binding the legs.

Over medium heat, deglaze the pan with the butter and add the mushrooms. Cook until the mushrooms are tender but not soggy, about 3 minutes. Remove from the heat.

Serve the quail hot with the creamy polenta and the sauce.

Fennel, Radicchio, and Orange Salad

1 head red radicchio (Treviso or Chioggia)

1 head green radicchio

1 bulb fresh fennel

1 bunch arugula (rocket)

2 medium navel oranges, peeled, cut into sections, membranes removed

3—4 tablespoons best quality extra-virgin olive oil

Salt and freshly ground black pepper to taste

In November the first navel oranges arrive from Sicily. The clean, cool taste of the fennel, the spiciness of the radicchio, and the sweet tang of the oranges make this a refreshing, palate-cleansing salad.

PLANNING AHEAD: The greens can be washed, dried, and wrapped in a clean, damp dish towel and put in the refrigerator hours in advance. The orange sections can be cut and put in a bowl in the refrigerator until serving.

Wash the radicchios and arugula thoroughly. Discard any wilted leaves and brown stems. Spin in a salad spinner to remove excess water. Tear or chop into small pieces. Put in a large salad bowl. Wash the fennel bulb and cut it in half. Remove the hard core and trim away any discolored outer layers. Slice the bulb into thin strips. Add to the salad along with the orange sections.

Toss with the olive oil, season with salt and pepper, and toss again. Serve.

Walnut-Leaf Pecorino with Corbezzolo Honey

1/2 small form (400 g) aged pecorino cheese that has been seasoned in walnut leaves

1/3 cup (80 ml) good-quality honey

2 firm ripe pears (Bosc or William)

1/2 lemon

8—10 walnut halves, to garnish

Tuscan-style bread, sliced

If you can find a pecorino (ewe's milk) cheese that has been aged in walnut, then it is worth every penny. If not, whatever your local cheesemonger has on offer that is a bit sharp and dry will work fine. A good Parmigiano-Reggiano (Italian parmesan) is always acceptable. In the fall in Tuscany a lovely accompaniment to pecorino cheese is a bitter, buttery honey made from the flowers of the strawberry tree (corbezzolo or arbutus). If corbezzolo honey is not available, then a chestnut, rosemary, lavender, or wildflower honey will do.

Wash and dry the pears. Cut them in half lengthwise, remove the stems and core. Thinly slice each half-pear and squeeze some lemon juice over the top to prevent them discoloring. Arrange the slices of pear in a fan pattern on a serving platter with slices of the pecorino cheese. Garnish with the walnut halves. Serve with the dish of honey and a basket of Tuscan bread.

Poached Quince Meringue Pie

POACHED QUINCE

6 quince, washed and scrubbed of outer "fur"

Juice of 1 lemon

1½ cups (300 g) sugar

1½ cups (375 ml) water

1½ cups (375 ml) dry white wine

Zest of 1 lemon (preferably organic), cut in wide strips

3 bay leaves

½ vanilla bean, split lengthwise

ASSEMBLING THE PIE

2 large eggs, separated

1 tablespoon cornstarch (cornflour)

⅛ teaspoon salt

⅛ teaspoon cream of tartar

⅓ cup (70 g) superfine (caster) sugar

1 recipe Shortcrust Pastry (see page 141)

My friend Miriam first introduced me to quince poached slowly in vanilla syrup until they turn a lovely ruby color. They are delicious straight from the oven with their crimson cooking syrup and a spoonful of plain yogurt or crème fraîche. The pie, with its contrasting tangy quince custard, flaky golden pastry and airy meringue, is a dessert worthy of the effort.

PLANNING AHEAD: The pie keeps for 2 days in the refrigerator. The quince take 3 hours to poach, and can be made a day or two in advance. The poached quince also freezes well for up to a month. The pastry dough can be made 2–3 days ahead of time.

POACHED QUINCE: Preheat the oven to 300°F/150°C/gas 2. Peel, quarter, and core the quince. Sprinkle the quarters of quince with the lemon juice to prevent them from turning brown as you work. Save the quince seeds, cores, and half the zest and put them in the center of a piece of clean cheesecloth (muslin). Tie the corners of the cloth to form a tight bundle. Put the quince in a single layer in the bottom of a large, high-sided baking dish with the cheesecloth bundle in the center. In a saucepan, dissolve the sugar in the water and bring to a boil. Remove from the heat. Add the wine. Pour the sugar wine syrup over the quince. Add the bay leaves, lemon zest, and vanilla bean. Cover with foil and bake for 3 hours, or until the quince are bright red and easily pierced with a knife and the syrup is the color of blood oranges. Set the pan on a cooling rack and allow to cool to room temperature (about 20 minutes).

ASSEMBLING AND BAKING THE TART: Increase oven temperature to 350°F/180°C/gas 4. If you are using quince poached from the day before, allow them to come to room temperature before using. Let the egg whites come to room temperature as well. Remove the cooked quince from the syrup with a slotted spoon and put them a medium-sized mixing bowl. Strain the syrup from the baking dish into a container for pouring on the tart later. Mash the quince with a fork until it is creamy. Add the egg yolks and cornstarch and mix well. Beat the egg whites with the salt and cream of tartar on high speed until soft peaks form. Add the sugar a tablespoon at a time. Beat until the egg whites form stiff shiny peaks.

Spread the quince mixture on the bottom of the cooled pastry shell. Top with the meringue. Bake for 20–25 minutes, or until the meringue is golden. Allow the tart to cool on a rack for 30 minutes before cutting. Put the quince syrup on the table so guests can help themselves if desired. Serve the pie with a dessert wine. Moscadello di Montalcino is a good choice.

A Parisian Valentine's Day

Oysters on the Half Shell
Clams and Mussels
Niçoise Salad
Onion and Chard Quiche
Tangy Lemon Tarts
Crêpes with Strawberries and Cointreau Whipped Cream

Wine suggestions: Veuve Clicquot Champagne,
Crémant de Loire sparkling rosé, or a Sauvignon Blanc

I like Paris in February when it's cold; there are fewer tourists
and the sidewalk cafés display trays of iced oysters on the half shell.
Give me fresh oysters and Champagne and I am happy for a week.

If you can't go to Paris for Valentine's Day, why not pretend?
This menu works for two or three couples, a small group of close friends,
or cut the recipes in half (and have nice leftovers in the case of the quiche)
for an intimate brunch for two. Play some Edith Piaf or Blossom Dearie
on the stereo and float through the day on a wave of French bubbles.

Oysters on the Half Shell

24 very fresh oysters in their shells

2 lemons, cut in wedges

Crushed ice, to serve

Tabasco or hot sauce, to serve

Fresh, live oysters that taste of clean sea foam do not need anything except perhaps a squeeze of fresh lemon juice and a little hot sauce. Slurp them down with a glass of cold champagne.

Rinse the oysters well to remove any sand and grit from the shells. Wear gloves to protect your hands. Grip the oyster in one hand with a clean dish towel. Use an oyster knife or clean flat screw driver to carefully pry open the oysters.

Loosen the oysters where they are attached to their shells so they will slip off easily. Set out a large platter with a raised lip. Cover it with ice. Arrange the oysters on their half shells on top of the ice. Decorate with a few wedges of lemon. Serve the Tabasco on the side.

Clams and Mussels

2 lb (1 kg) fresh clams

2 lb (1 kg) fresh mussels

1 tablespoon coarse sea salt

2 tablespoons extra-virgin olive oil

2 tablespoons butter

Generous pinch of red pepper flakes

4 cloves garlic, minced

Freshly ground black pepper to taste

2 tablespoons finely chopped Italian flat-leaf parsley

4 tablespoons dry white wine

Juice of 1 lemon

1 lemon, cut into 6 wedges, for garnish

Crusty baguettes (French loaves), to serve

PLANNING AHEAD: The clams and mussels can be cleaned, soaked, and drained the night before. Store them in a large bowl in the refrigerator overnight. Rinse and drain in a colander before using the next day.

Rinse the clams and mussels in cold water and scrub their shells with wire wool. Remove the beards from the mussels. Soak the scrubbed shellfish in a large bowl (or clean sink) of cold water with the sea salt for 1 hour. Drain well.

Heat the olive oil with the butter in a large pot with a lid over medium-high heat. Add the pepper flakes and garlic and sauté for 30 seconds. Add the clams and mussels and stir well. Crack some pepper into the pot, add the parsley, and then pour in the wine. Cover and cook for 8–10 minutes. After 5 minutes, check to see if most of the shells have opened and give them a stir. Cover and cook for a few minutes more. Discard any clams or mussels that have not opened after 10 minutes. Drizzle the lemon juice over the shells. Ladle the shellfish into bowls with the cooking juice.

Serve with an extra wedge of lemon and slices of crusty baguette. Don't be afraid to use your fingers to scoop up some of the broth with the shells.

Niçoise Salad

DRESSING

2 cloves garlic

½ teaspoon whole black peppercorns

1 salted anchovy, rinsed and cleaned into 2 fillets

2 tablespoons fresh lemon juice

½ cup (125 ml) extra-virgin olive oil

2 tablespoons finely chopped Italian flat-leaf parsley

1 tablespoon fresh thyme leaves

1 tablespoon finely chopped chives

Salt to taste

SALAD

1 lb (500 g) waxy baby potatoes (Bintje, Desiree, or Kipfler), scrubbed

1 lb (500 g) haricot green beans, washed and ends trimmed

2 handfuls cherry tomatoes, weighing about 1½ cups (375 g), cut in half

1 lb (500 g) thick, very fresh tuna fillet (a loin, in a log shape)

1 head curly endive lettuce

1 head escarole lettuce

1 head butter lettuce

A handful of Kalamata olives

3 hard-boiled eggs, peeled and cut into wedges

3 salted anchovies, rinsed and cleaned into 6 fillets

PLANNING AHEAD: The dressing can be made and the lettuces can be washed in advance, but the salad is best when the potatoes, tuna, and green beans are still lukewarm.

DRESSING: In a large mortar, crush the garlic with the peppercorns and anchovy into a thick paste. Add the lemon juice and mix well. Stir constantly with the pestle as you slowly pour in the olive oil. If your mortar is too small to hold the oil, then transfer the mixture to a bowl and whisk in the oil. Stir in the parsley, thyme and chives. Taste for salt.

SALAD: Boil the potatoes whole in their skins in a large pot of salted water until they are easily pierced with a fork but not falling apart. Drain. When the potatoes are cool enough to handle, slip off their skins. Leave the small baby potatoes whole, or if using slightly larger potatoes, cut them in half crosswise.

Cook the green beans in a pot of boiling salted water. Parboil until they can be pierced with a fork but are still a bit al dente. Drain. Toss the green beans with the tomatoes and a few tablespoons of the dressing.

Heat 1 tablespoon of olive oil in a large skillet (frying pan) over medium-high heat. When the oil is smoking hot, add the tuna loin. Sear quickly on all sides, turning the loin with wooden spoons. The outside of the tuna should be brown but the inside should be bright red and rare. This will take about 1 minute. Remove the tuna from the pan and place on a cutting board to cool.

Wash and spin dry all the lettuces. Tear them into bite-sized pieces. Toss the lettuces with a bit of dressing in the largest, shallowest salad bowl you have. Add the potatoes and sprinkle with the olives. Slice the tuna loin into ¼-inch (5-mm) thick medallions and add to the salad. Drizzle some of the dressing over the potatoes, tuna, and olives. Add the green beans, tomatoes, eggs, and anchovies. Toss the salad well and serve lukewarm.

Onion and Chard Quiche

1 recipe Whole-Wheat Pastry (see page 141)

FILLING

4 tablespoons unsalted butter

4 large yellow onions, quartered and thinly sliced

$\frac{1}{2}$ teaspoon salt

8 oz (250 g) baby Swiss chard leaves, washed, trimmed of all tough stems, and coarsely chopped

2 large eggs

2 egg yolks

1 cup (250 ml) Half & Half or $\frac{1}{2}$ cup (125 ml) heavy (double) cream and $\frac{1}{2}$ cup (125 ml) whole milk

1 teaspoon Dijon mustard

$\frac{1}{4}$ teaspoon freshly ground black pepper

2 teaspoons fresh thyme leaves

$\frac{1}{8}$ teaspoon nutmeg

$\frac{1}{8}$ teaspoon cayenne pepper

$\frac{1}{8}$ teaspoon salt

1 cup (125 g) grated Swiss cheese (Emmental)

PLANNING AHEAD: This quiche lasts for 4 days in the refrigerator, and it is good reheated.

Use a 10-inch (25-cm) quiche dish or baking dish with 2-inch (5-cm) sides. On a floured surface, roll out the pastry into a 13-inch (33-cm), $\frac{1}{8}$-inch (3-mm) thick circle. Line the pan with the pastry. Crimp the edges and prick with a fork. Refrigerate for 20–30 minutes.

FILLING: In a large skillet (frying pan) over medium heat, melt the butter. Add the onions and coat well in the butter. Sprinkle with salt. Turn down the heat to low, cover the pan and slowly sweat the onions for 30 minutes, or until they are very soft and sweet to the taste. Stir and check the temperature occasionally to make sure the onions do not brown.

When the onions are soft, add the chard to the pan. Add it in batches as it wilts down. Increase the heat to medium and cook for 5 minutes. Let the mixture cool to room temperature.

Preheat the oven to 400°F/200°C/gas 6.

Bake the pastry blind for 10 minutes. Uncover and bake for another 10 minutes, or until golden. Cool on a rack until egg mixture is ready.

Reduce the oven temperature to 350°F/180°C/gas 4.

In a large bowl, whisk together the eggs, egg yolks, cream, milk, mustard, pepper, thyme, nutmeg, cayenne and salt. Add the cooled onion and chard mixture (scrape all the juices from the pan into the bowl as well) and top with the cheese. Stir well.

Fill the pastry shell with the egg mixture. Bake for 45 minutes, or until the quiche is golden brown on top and set. Cool on a rack for 10 minutes. Serve hot or at room temperature.

Tangy Lemon Tarts

1 recipe Sweet Egg Pastry (see page 141)

LEMON CUSTARD

3 egg yolks

½ cup (100 g) Vanilla Sugar (see page 140)

Finely grated zest of 2 large lemons, preferably organic

6 tablespoons fresh lemon juice

6 tablespoons heavy (double) cream

Shredded lemon zest, to garnish

Whipped cream (optional)

PLANNING AHEAD: The tarts can be made up to 3–4 days in advance and stored in the refrigerator.

Set out six 3½-inch (9-cm) mini tart pans. Butter the pans. If the tart pans do not have removable bottoms, cut small circles of waxed paper to line the bottoms and butter the paper.

Divide the pastry into six balls. On a floured surface roll each ball into a 5-inch (13-cm) circle. Line the tart pans with the pastry. Press the pastry into place with your thumbs if it cracks or breaks. Trim and crimp the edges of the pastry. Prick all over with a fork. Put the tart pans on a baking sheet. Refrigerate for 30 minutes.

Preheat the oven to 400°F/200°C/gas 6. Cover the pastry in each pan with waxed paper and fill with dried beans or pie weights. Bake the pastry blind for 10 minutes. Remove the paper and beans or weights. Bake for 10 minutes more, After 5 minutes check to see if any large air bubbles are forming in the pastry and if so, prick them with a fork. Bake until the pastry shells are golden. Cool on a wire rack. Do not remove the baked pastry shells from the pans as they are too fragile to withstand the unbaked custard.

Reduce the oven temperature to 250°F/130°C/gas ½.

LEMON CUSTARD: Use a wire whisk to beat the egg yolks and vanilla sugar until pale and creamy. Whisk in the lemon juice and zest, and then the cream. Transfer to a jug so the mixture can be poured easily. Fill the tart shells with the lemon custard as full as possible.

Bake for 20–25 minutes. The tarts will be soft-set, slightly wobbly and bubbly in the center and pale golden brown at the edges when they are done. The tarts will continue to firm up as they cool. Cool the tarts on a wire rack for one hour. Serve at room temperature, or refrigerate until ready to serve.

Gently squeeze the sides of the tart pans to loosen and release the tarts from the sides. Carefully invert to unmold. Garnish with the shredded lemon zest and serve with whipped cream, if liked.

Crêpes with Strawberries and Cointreau Whipped Cream

CRÊPE BATTER

1 cup (250 ml) milk

½ cup (125 ml) cold water

3 egg yolks

1 tablespoon Vanilla Sugar (see page 140)

3 tablespoons Cointreau

1 teaspoon finely grated orange zest

⅛ teaspoon salt

1 cup (150 g) all-purpose (plain) flour

5 tablespoons unsalted butter, melted

STRAWBERRY COMPOTE

4 tablespoons granulated sugar

4 tablespoons balsamic vinegar

2 tablespoons finely grated orange zest

½ teaspoon freshly ground black pepper

2 lb (1 kg) fresh strawberries, cut in half lengthwise

COINTREAU WHIPPED CREAM

1 cup (250 ml) heavy (double) cream

2 tablespoons Cointreau

Shredded orange zest, to garnish

PLANNING AHEAD: The crêpe batter needs to be refrigerated for at least 2 hours before using. The cooked crêpes can be made hours before serving and stacked between sheets of waxed paper. They can also be made the day before and stored between layers of waxed paper in an airtight container in the refrigerator, or frozen for up to a month.

CRÊPE BATTER: Place all the ingredients in a food processor or blender. Blend on high speed for 1 minute. Scrape the sides of the blender with a spatula and blend for 30 seconds more. Pour the batter into a covered container and refrigerate for at least 2 hours, or overnight.

STRAWBERRY COMPOTE: In a small bowl, dissolve the sugar in the balsamic vinegar to taste. The mixture should be sweet with a tangy finish. Stir in the orange zest and black pepper. Toss the strawberries with the sauce and let macerate for 1 hour.

Heat a 9-inch (23-cm) crêpe pan over a moderately high heat. Melt a small pat of butter in the pan to coat the surface. When the pan is very hot and the butter is beginning to brown and smoke, ladle about 4 tablespoons of the batter into the pan. Quickly tilt the pan in all directions to spread the batter in a thin, circular film across the bottom. When the edges of the crêpe have begun to curl up slightly and turn golden brown, loosen the edges with the spatula and flip over. Cook briefly on the other side. This whole process should take about 30 seconds. Stack the cooked crêpes between waxed paper. Repeat until all the batter is used.

Wait to assemble the crêpes until ready to serve.

COINTREAU WHIPPED CREAM: Whip the cream with the Cointreau into firm peaks.

Spoon some of the strawberry compôte onto the center of a crêpe. Layer with some of the whipped cream and roll. Arrange the rolled crêpes on a platter or individual serving plates. Garnish with the shredded orange zest and a few extra strawberries. Serve.

Metropolitan

Cappuccinos
Nutty Spicy Nicey
Bloody Marys
Smoked Salmon and Chive Omelets
Borscht
Poppy Seed Rolls
Spinach Salad
Blue Waldorf Salad
Cheesecake with Berries

This menu was created for those dreary, drizzly sunless Sundays in the city.
A day that is only suitable for an afternoon visit to the museum, a matinee,
or a long, casual brunch with friends. I have chosen several dishes with
bright colors and warming spices to contrast the gray weather.

Cappuccinos

8 shots of espresso, or one pot of dark coffee
   from a large Italian Moka

1¾ cups (430 ml) hot milk

A sugar bowl

If you do not have a home espresso machine, an Italian metal stove top coffeemaker called a "Moka" (Bialetti is a good brand) is a fine substitute. Froth the milk with steam from the espresso machine or with a handheld milk frother available at most kitchen supply stores

Use small cappuccino/tea cups that have ²/₃ cup (150 ml) capacity (not the bucket-sized cups you see in Starbucks). Pour approximately one shot of espresso into each cup, or divide the Moka coffee evenly among the cups. Add about 3–4 tablespoons of hot milk to each cup, and then use a spoon to float some milk foam on top. Serve hot with a sugar bowl on the side.

Nutty Spicy Nicey

2½ cups (375 g) all-purpose (plain) flour

½ teaspoon salt

I teaspoon ground cinnamon

I teaspoon ground ginger

½ teaspoon ground cardamom

¼ teaspoon nutmeg

⅛ teaspoon allspice

1½ cups (300 g) firmly packed soft brown sugar

¾ cup (180 g) cold unsalted butter, cut into chunks

I cup (150 g) coarsely chopped nuts (any combination of pistachios, pecans, hazelnuts, or walnuts)

⅓ cup (50 g) flaked almonds

I tablespoon baking powder

½ teaspoon baking soda (bicarbonate of soda)

2 eggs, lightly beaten

1¼ cups (310 ml) buttermilk (or milk with I tablespoon lemon juice—let stand for 5 minutes)

I teaspoon vanilla extract (essence)

I ripe but firm Bosc pear

PLANNING AHEAD: Also known as Pear streusel, this coffeecake is best eaten the day it is made. If making in advance, omit the pear, as the moisture it produces will eventually make the cake gummy.

Preheat the oven to 350°F/180°C/gas 4. Butter a 13 x 9-inch (33 x 23-cm) baking pan. Line the pan with baking paper. Butter the paper.

In a large bowl, mix the flour, salt, spices, and brown sugar with a fork. Cut in the butter with a pastry cutter or work with your fingers until the mixture resembles coarse bread crumbs. Take out 1½ cups (275 g) of the mixture and put in a medium bowl with the nuts and flaked almonds and set aside (this is the streusel topping).

Add the baking powder and soda to the mixture remaining in the large bowl and stir well with a fork. In a separate bowl, mix the wet ingredients (buttermilk, eggs, and vanilla). Make a well in the dry ingredients and add the wet ingredients all at once. Stir to just combine. The mixture will have small lumps.

Peel, core, and thinly slice the pear lengthwise. Pour the batter into the prepared pan. Arrange the pear slices in a single layer on the surface. Cover with the reserved streusel mixture. Bake for 45–55 minutes, or until the cake is deep golden brown and a toothpick inserted into the center comes out clean. Cool on a rack for 15–20 minutes. Serve warm or at room temperature.

Bloody Marys

¾ cup (180 ml) fresh lime juice

1½ tablespoons fresh horseradish

3 tablespoons Worcestershire sauce

1 clove garlic, crushed

¾ teaspoon Tabasco sauce
   (1 teaspoon if you like it extra spicy)

¾ teaspoon celery salt

1 teaspoon freshly ground black pepper

1¼ quarts (1.25 liters) chilled tomato juice

1¼ cups (310 ml) vodka

Ice

Celery stalks with leaves, to garnish

PLANNING AHEAD: The Bloody Mary mix can be 2–3 days in advance and stored in the refrigerator.

In a large pitcher, mix the lime juice with the sauces and spices. Stir with a wooden spoon as you add the tomato juice. Blend well. Adjust seasonings to your liking.

Fill six tall glasses with ice. Add 3 tablespoons of vodka to each glass. Top with the tomato mixture. Stir. Garnish with the celery. Serve chilled.

Smoked Salmon and Chive Omelets

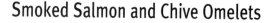

6–8 oz (180–250 g) smoked salmon

12–16 eggs (2 eggs per omelet)

6–8 tablespoons finely chopped chives

½ teaspoon mustard powder

⅛ teaspoon cayenne

Salt and freshly ground black pepper to taste

4 tablespoons butter

Snipped chives, to garnish

PLANNING AHEAD: Each omelet takes 1 minute to cook. Either cook individual omelets and serve immediately, or keep warm in a buttered dish in a warm oven until all the omelets are cooked.

In a large bowl, beat the eggs with a fork until just combined. Add the chives, mustard powder, cayenne, salt, and pepper and mix briefly.

Heat a large nonstick skillet (frying pan) over medium-high heat until it is very hot. Melt a small pat of butter in the pan and swirl to coat the bottom. Pour two eggs worth of the egg mixture into the pan (this will make a very thin layer). Add 1 oz (30 g) of smoked salmon. Use a rubber spatula to loosen the sides, shaking the pan to ensure the bottom is not sticking. Fold two sides of the egg circle toward the middle (making a long rectangular envelope shape). Then tilt the pan and roll the omelet over with the spatula (or flip in the air with the flick of your wrist). Cook for a few more seconds. The omelet should be golden on the outside and creamy inside. The whole process will take about 1 minute.

Slide the omelet hot from the pan onto an individual serving plate, or transfer to a buttered dish in a warm oven until all the omelets are cooked. Garnish each omelet with the snipped chives and a small grinding of black pepper.

Smoked Salmon and Chive Omelets with Bloody Mary

Borscht

1 large onion, chopped

2 large stalks celery, chopped

1 large carrot, peeled and chopped

Pinch of red pepper flakes

1 teaspoon caraway seeds

2 tablespoons extra-virgin olive oil

1 bay leaf

2 tablespoons finely chopped parsley

3 cloves garlic, minced

A handful of chopped fresh dill leaves

1 lb (500 g) white cabbage, chopped

2 lb (1 kg) potatoes, peeled and cut into cubes

1 lb (500 g) beets (beetroot), peeled and coarsely chopped

1 teaspoon salt

1 teaspoon freshly ground black pepper

1½ quarts (1.5 liters) Quick Stock (see page 138)

14 oz (400 g) canned whole, peeled tomatoes

Sour cream, to garnish

A few sprigs of fresh dill, to garnish

PLANNING AHEAD: The borscht lasts for 3–4 days in the refrigerator, or it can be frozen for up to a month.

In a large 6-quart (6-liter) pot over medium heat, sauté the onion, celery, carrot, red pepper flakes, and caraway seeds in the olive oil. Cook for 10 minutes, stirring frequently. The vegetables should be softened but not browned. Add the bay leaf, parsley, garlic, dill, and cabbage. Sauté for 5 minutes, or until the cabbage is wilted and half its original bulk. Add the potatoes, beets, salt, pepper, and stock. Bring to a boil and then simmer, covered, for 30 minutes.

After 30 minutes, add the tomatoes. Crush the tomatoes between your fingers as you add them to the soup. Continue to simmer on low heat for another 30 minutes, partially covered.

Discard the bay leaf. In a blender with a tightly fitting lid, purée the soup in batches (be careful when blending hot liquids). Blend until the borscht is free of lumps, but still has a bit of texture. You do not want it to be completely smooth. Taste for salt and pepper. Serve hot with a dollop of sour cream and a small piece of fresh dill on top.

Poppy Seed Rolls

1 recipe Sweet Roll Dough (see page 140)

4 tablespoons milk

3 tablespoons poppy seeds

½ teaspoon salt

PLANNING AHEAD: Make the Sweet Roll Dough the day before. Place in the baking pan, cover, and refrigerate overnight. The next morning bring to room temperature and let rise for 1½ hours before baking.

Butter a 15 x 10-inch (35 x 25-cm) baking sheet with 1-inch (2.5-cm) sides. Knead the risen dough on a well-floured surface for a few minutes until it is smooth and elastic. Dust your hands and the dough with flour as needed. The dough should be stretchy, like pizza dough.

Roll and pat the dough into a large rectangle and press it into the baking tray. At this point either cover and refrigerate overnight to bake the next morning, or cover with a damp dish towel and let rise for 1 hour.

Preheat the oven to 350°F/180°C/gas 4. Use a pizza cutter to cut a the risen dough into twenty 2-inch (5-cm) square rolls. Brush the surface with the milk. Sprinkle the surface with the poppy seeds and salt. Bake for 25 minutes, or until puffed and golden brown on top. Cool on a rack for 10 minutes. Serve warm with the borscht.

Borscht with **Poppy Seed Rolls**

Spinach Salad

CROUTONS (see page 139)

DRESSING

4 tablespoons extra-virgin olive oil

1 clove garlic, crushed

1 tablespoon balsamic vinegar

1 tablespoon Dijon mustard

1 tablespoon honey

Salt and freshly ground black pepper to taste

SALAD

1 lb (500 g) fresh spinach, washed,
   trimmed of tough stems and spun dry

1/2 cup (60 g) bacon, chopped

2 hard-boiled eggs, chopped

2 green onions (spring onions), chopped

PLANNING AHEAD: The croutons and the dressing can be made in advance.

To make the dressing, put all the ingredients in a small bowl and whisk until well combined. Taste for salt and pepper.

Cook the bacon in a large skillet (frying pan) until crisp and brown. Drain on paper towels.

Put the spinach in a large salad bowl. Top with the bacon, egg, green onion, and half the croutons. Pour the dressing over the salad and toss well. Serve with the remaining croutons passed separately.

Blue Waldorf Salad

2 firm, ripe pears (Williams, Bosc, or Bartlet)

4 or 5 tart, crunchy apples
   (Pink Rose, Granny Smith, Gala, or Fuji)

Juice of 1 lemon

2 stalks celery, finely chopped

1 green onion (spring onion), finely chopped

1 tablespoon finely chopped Italian flat-leaf parsley

3 tablespoons crumbled dry, spicy Gorgonzola or
   Roquefort cheese

1 cup (250 ml) plain low-fat yogurt

2 teaspoons poppy seeds

1/2 cup (75 g) chopped toasted walnuts

Freshly ground black pepper to taste

2 cups (200 g) finely shredded purple cabbage or
   Chioggia radicchio

PLANNING AHEAD: This salad can be made 2–3 hours in advance stored in the refrigerator.

If the apples and pears are organic, leave their skins on as they provide a nice color effect in the salad. Core the apples and pears, cut into 2-inch (5-cm) pieces, and toss in a large bowl with the lemon juice. Add the celery, green onion, parsley, blue cheese, yogurt, poppy seeds, and walnuts. Mix well. Season with pepper to taste.

In a large salad bowl, make a bed of the shredded cabbage or radicchio and put the Waldorf in the middle.

Cheesecake with Berries

CRUST

3/4 cup (100 g) finely chopped almonds

1/2 cup (50 g) crushed amaretti cookies

1 cup (100 g) crushed graham crackers or digestive biscuits

Scant 1/2 cup (100 g) melted butter

FILLING

2 lb (1 kg) cream cheese, at room temperature

1 1/2 cups (300 g) Vanilla Sugar (see page 140)

1/4 teaspoon almond extract (essence)

2 teaspoons vanilla extract (essence)

6 eggs, at room temperature

TOPPING

1 3/4 cups (430 ml) sour cream

2 tablespoons Vanilla Sugar (see page 140)

1 teaspoon vanilla extract (essence)

2 cups (250 g) fresh berries (raspberries, blueberries, or red currants—or a combination of all three)

PLANNING AHEAD: Make the cheesecake the day before and chill overnight. It keeps for 5 days in the refrigerator without the berries and 2–3 days once the berries have been added.

Preheat the oven to 375°F/190°C/gas 5. Butter the sides, but not the bottom, of a 9-inch (23-cm) springform pan. In a large bowl, mix the almonds, cracker and amaretti crumbs, and melted butter until well combined. Press the crust mixture into the bottom and sides of the pan. The buttered sides will help the crumb mixture to stick to the sides of the pan, but the crust will be thicker on the bottom. Bake for 10 minutes, or until golden brown. Cool completely on a rack.

Reduce the oven temperature to 300°F/150°C/gas 2.

In a large bowl, beat the cream cheese, vanilla sugar, and extracts on medium-high speed until the mixture is creamy and lump-free. Add the eggs, one at a time, beating on medium-low speed just long enough to combine each egg into the mixture. Be careful not to over beat (as over beating toughens the texture of the cake).

Place the pan with the cooled crust on a large baking sheet (the baking sheet supports the weight of the cake and makes it easier to pull the pan in and out of the oven without accidents). Pour the cream cheese mixture into the cooled crust. Bake for about 1 hour. When done, the cheesecake should be soft-set (slightly wobbly in the middle but not totally liquid) and the surface should have a dull sheen. Turn off the oven and leave to cool in the oven with the door ajar for 1 hour. The gradual cooling of the cake in the oven will reduce the number of cracks on the surface, but do not worry if a few cracks form because the topping will cover them.

Remove the cheesecake from the oven to a cooling rack. Preheat the oven to 300°F/150°C/gas 2. Add the sugar and vanilla extract to the sour cream and stir well. Pour the sour cream mixture on top of the cheesecake and smooth it with the back of a spoon or rubber spatula to cover the surface. Bake for 10 minutes. Cool on a rack.

Run a knife around the edge of the pan and then gently release the sides of the springform. Refrigerate overnight. Decorate the top with the berries before serving.

Pacific Northwest

Dark Roasted Coffee
Mimosas
Cranberry Hazelnut Cinnamon Rolls
Crab Cakes with Roasted Red Pepper Sauce
Corn and Sweet Potato Chowder
Poached Salmon
Mixed Baby Greens with Pears and Blue Cheese
Poached Eggs on Wilted Spinach
and Garlic Sourdough Bread
Hedgehog Potatoes
Creamy Apple Tart

*Wine suggestions: Argyle sparkling wine or Sauvignon
Blanc, Willamette Valley Chardonnay,
Chehalem Pinot Noir*

I have several good friends who live on the Olympic Peninsula in Washington,
and I always eat incredibly well whenever I visit. The Pacific Northwest is well known for
its fresh salmon, crab, shellfish, berries, hazelnuts, apples, wild greens and herbs,
and award winning local wines. Pike Street market in Seattle is a joy for any cook to visit,
with its numerous stalls of fresh fish, fruits, and vegetables. Starbucks, Peet's, and
Seattle's Best all began their coffee-roasting businesses here, and Seattle locals are
known for their love of (and insistence upon) excellent coffee. Seattle and Portland
are fast becoming famous for their innovative restaurants that emphasize seasonal,
local products. This menu has a few of my Northwest favorites.

Mimosas

Dry sparkling wine, chilled

Freshly squeezed orange juice

Fresh strawberries, to garnish (optional)

Fill a champagne flute ¾ full of cold sparkling wine for each guest. Top with a splash of orange juice. Make a small cut upward from the bottom of each strawberry, so that it will sit on the side of the glass. Serve.

Cranberry Hazelnut Cinnamon Rolls

I recipe Sweet Bread Roll Dough (see page 140)

FILLING

I cup (100 g) fresh cranberries (or thawed frozen)

3 tablespoons water

½ cup (100 g) firmly packed brown sugar

I teaspoon cinnamon

⅓ cup (40 g) chopped toasted hazelnuts

I tablespoon finely grated orange zest

4 tablespoons unsalted butter, very soft

ORANGE ICING

⅓ cup (50 g) confectioners' (icing) sugar

I teaspoon finely grated orange zest

I tablespoon fresh orange juice

PLANNING AHEAD: The rolls take 3 hours to make (2 hours rising time). They can be formed, but not allowed to rise, the day before. Put the cut slices in the buttered pans, cover with plastic wrap, and refrigerate. The next morning, take the pans out of the refrigerator and allow 1½ hours for the rolls to rise and come to room temperature before baking.

FILLING: Put the cranberries and water in a saucepan and bring to a boil. When the cranberries begin to burst (about 2 minutes), remove from the heat. Cool and drain, reserving the juice for another use. In a separate bowl, mix the brown sugar, cinnamon, hazelnuts, and orange zest with a fork.

ASSEMBLE AND BAKE: Butter two 9 x 2-inch (23 x 5-cm) round springform pans. Turn the dough out onto a well-floured surface and pat or roll it into a 12 to 14-inch (30 to 35-cm) square (the dough should be ½ inch (1-cm) thick). Spread with the butter. Sprinkle half the sugar and nut mixture on top, dot with the cranberries, and finish with the remaining sugar and nut mixture.

Roll the dough into a log, pinching the ends and the seam to seal. With a large knife, trim 1-inch (2.5-cm) off each end of the roll and discard. Cut crosswise into 1-inch (2.5-cm) thick slices. Place the slices cut-side up in the buttered pans. Place one slice in the center of each pan with 5 or 6 slices not too closely spaced around it.

Cover the pans with a clean towel and put in a warm place to rise for 1 hour.

Preheat the oven to 350°F/180°C/gas 4. Bake for 30–35 minutes, until puffed and golden brown. Cool on a rack for 5 minutes. Release the sides of the pans. The rolls will be stuck together to form a round cake of swirling spirals.

ORANGE ICING: Stir the confectioners' sugar and orange juice and zest with a fork until smooth. Drizzle the icing over the warm cakes. Serve the cakes warm and let guests pull off the rolls.

Crab Cakes

8 oz (250 g) crabmeat (Dungeness if available)

1 tablespoon extra-virgin olive oil

$\frac{1}{2}$ medium red onion, finely chopped

1 celery stalk, finely diced

2 cups (120 g) soft white bread crumbs (no crusts)

2 tablespoons finely chopped Italian flat-leaf parsley

$\frac{1}{2}$ teaspoon finely chopped fresh thyme

1 green onion (spring onion), white and green parts
    finely chopped

4 tablespoons mayonnaise

1 teaspoon Dijon mustard

1 egg, lightly beaten

Pinch of cayenne pepper

A couple shakes of Tabasco

1 tablespoon dry sherry

Salt and freshly ground black pepper to taste

$\frac{3}{4}$ cup (90 g) fine, dry bread crumbs
    (Japanese Panko crumbs if available) to coat

1 recipe Roasted Red Pepper Sauce (recipe follows), to garnish

PLANNING AHEAD: The crab mixture can be formed into cakes and refrigerated for hours in advance. Just pop in the oven before serving.

Pick through the crabmeat and remove any bits of shell. Heat the olive oil in a large skillet over medium heat. Sauté the onion and celery until soft and translucent, but do not let it brown. Remove from the heat and cool.

In a large bowl, combine all the ingredients, except the dry bread crumbs, and mix well. Lightly oil a large baking tray. Form the crab mixture into cakes about $2\frac{1}{2}$ inches (9 cm) in diameter. Roll and pat the cakes in the dry bread crumbs to cover them completely. Place the cakes on the tray and refrigerate for at least 20 minutes.

Put the tray of chilled crab cakes under a hot broiler (grill) in the oven. Watch them carefully. Toast to golden brown on the top, then turn over and grill the other side until golden brown. Serve the hot crab cakes with a dollop of the Roasted Red Pepper Sauce.

Roasted Red Pepper Sauce

3 red bell peppers (capsicums)

Pinch of red pepper flakes

1 clove garlic, crushed

$\frac{1}{4}$ cup (45 g) toasted pine nuts

1 tablespoon lemon juice

2–4 tablespoons extra-virgin olive oil

Salt and freshly ground black pepper to taste

Roast the peppers over the open flame of a gas burner until charred and completely black on all sides. Put the charred peppers in a paper bag, or in a large glass bowl covered with plastic wrap, to cool. When the peppers are cool, the skins will slip off easily. Try to remove the blackened skin without using water—or very little. Remove the stem, white membranes, and the seeds.

Put the roasted peppers in a blender or food processor with the red pepper flakes, garlic, pine nuts, lemon juice, and 2 tablespoons of olive oil. Blend at high speed until smooth. If the mixture is too thick to blend properly, add a bit more oil. Taste for salt and pepper.

Crab Cakes with Roasted Red Pepper Sauce

Corn and Sweet Potato Chowder

3½ oz (100 g) smoked bacon, diced

2 leeks, white and pale green part only, finely chopped

3 shallots, finely chopped

2 stalks celery, finely chopped

2 tablespoons butter

1 bay leaf

2 cloves garlic, minced

3 medium potatoes, weighing about 12 oz (350 g), peeled and cut into 1-inch (2.5-cm) cubes

1 lb (500 g) sweet potatoes, peeled and cut into 1-inch (2.5-cm) cubes

2 cups (300 g) fresh sweet corn kernels (or canned)

3 tablespoons dry sherry

6 tablespoons dry white wine

3 tablespoons minced Italian flat-leaf parsley

1 tablespoon fresh thyme

½ teaspoon salt

1 teaspoon freshly ground black pepper

⅛ teaspoon cayenne pepper

1¼ quarts (1.25 liters) Quick Stock (see page 138)

4 tablespoons heavy (double) cream

Chopped parsley, to garnish

PLANNING AHEAD: This soup is even better the next day. It lasts for 3–4 days in the refrigerator.

Cook the bacon in a large soup pot over medium heat until it turns brown and has released its fat. Add the leeks, shallots, celery, and butter. Sauté gently for 5–10 minutes, reducing the heat if the leeks and shallots threaten to brown. Add the bay leaf, garlic, potatoes, sweet potatoes, and corn. Stir well. Cook for 5–10 minutes, stirring frequently. Pour in the sherry and wine. Cook for 3–5 minutes over medium heat to reduce the wine. Add the herbs, spices, and stock. Bring to a boil and then reduce to low heat.

Simmer, partially covered, for 1 hour, or until the potatoes are tender and easily pierced with a fork but still holding their shape. Stir in the cream. Taste for salt and seasoning. Serve hot with a sprinkle of parsley on top.

Poached Salmon

4 lb (2 kg) fresh, whole wild salmon

3–4 cloves garlic, thinly sliced

A large handful fresh dill leaves

6 tablespoons butter, cut in flakes

1/2 teaspoon freshly ground black pepper

1/2 teaspoon sea salt

6 tablespoons dry white wine

2 lemons, cut into thin wedges, to garnish

Extra fresh dill leaves, to garnish

Serve the salmon warm. It is also delicious served cold the next day.

Preheat the oven to 350°F/180°C/gas 4. Butter a baking dish large enough to hold the salmon. Rinse the salmon and pat dry with paper towels. Cut deep crosswise slits every 2 inches (5 cm) along both sides of the salmon. Put the salmon in the baking dish. Pack the slits and the cavity of the salmon with the garlic, dill, and pieces of butter. Season the fish with pepper and salt. Pour the wine into the dish. Cover with aluminum foil, sealing the edges to keep in all the steam.

Bake for 20 minutes. Gently turn the fish over with wooden spoons. Spoon some of the juices over the top. Reseal the foil and bake for 20–30 minutes more. After 20 minutes, test the salmon for doneness with a fork. It will flake away easily from the bone when done.

Transfer the salmon to a serving platter. Drizzle with the cooking juices and squeeze half a lemon over the top. Garnish with the lemon and dill. Cut along the backbone and slide pieces off the bone.

Mixed Baby Greens with Pears and Blue Cheese

GLAZED WALNUTS

4 tablespoons sugar

1 tablespoon water

1/4 teaspoon salt

1/4 teaspoon freshly ground black pepper

1 cup (100 g) coarsely chopped walnuts

RASPBERRY DRESSING

1/2 cup (125 g) fresh raspberries or 1/4 cup (60 g) thawed

4 tablespoons extra-virgin olive oil

1 tablespoon balsamic vinegar

1 teaspoon sugar

1 clove garlic, crushed

1 teaspoon lemon juice

1/4 teaspoon salt

1/4 teaspoon freshly ground black pepper

2 teaspoons finely chopped fresh chives

SALAD

12 cups (400 g) assorted baby salad greens

1 firm-ripe pear

1/3 cup (45 g) crumbled blue cheese (Gorgonzola or Roquefort)

PLANNING AHEAD: The glazed walnuts and the dressing can be made the day before.

GLAZED WALNUTS: Put the sugar, water, salt, and pepper in a skillet (frying pan) over medium heat. Cook until the sugar has caramelized and is dark brown, about 5 minutes. Add the walnuts and stir until well coated. Transfer the walnuts to a piece of waxed paper to cool. When cool, break any large clusters into bite-sized pieces.

DRESSING: Put all the ingredients except the chives in a blender. Blend on medium speed until the mixture is smooth. Whisk in the chives.

Wash and spin dry all the baby lettuces. Core and slice the pears thinly lengthwise. Cut each slice in half.

In a large salad bowl, toss the salad greens and pear with the dressing. Top with the blue cheese and the glazed walnuts. Serve.

Poached Salmon with **Mixed Baby Greens with Pears and Blue Cheese**

Poached Eggs on Wilted Spinach and Garlic Sourdough Toast

3 lb (1.5 kg) fresh spinach leaves, washed and tough stems removed, coarsely chopped

3 tablespoons extra-virgin olive oil

1/8 teaspoon red pepper flakes

3 cloves garlic, thinly sliced

Salt and freshly ground black pepper to taste

6–12 fresh eggs

1 tablespoon white wine vinegar

12 thick slices of crusty sourdough bread

1 clove garlic, peeled

4 tablespoons butter

2 tablespoons finely grated parmesan

Salt and freshly ground black pepper to taste

This dish is really a lighter, spicier Eggs Florentine, minus the heavy hollandaise. If making the whole menu, then serve one poached egg per person. Otherwise plan on two eggs per person.

In a large skillet, heat the olive oil with the red pepper flakes over medium heat. Add the garlic and sauté lightly for 15–20 seconds. Do not let the garlic brown. Add the spinach in batches, stirring and adding more as it wilts down. Cover and cook for 3–5 minutes, or just long enough for the spinach to be tender but not mushy. Add salt and pepper to taste. Remove from the heat and keep covered.

Bring 2-inches (5-cm) of water to boil in a large, high-sided skillet or wide saucepan. Pour the vinegar into the simmering water. Make a vortex in the water with a wooden spoon. Crack an egg close to the surface of the water and slip it in. Use the wooden spoon to gently lap any spreading egg white back towards the yolk. It is easiest to cook eggs in batches, so 2 or 3 at a time. Cook until the whites are opaque (about 2 minutes). Remove the egg with a slotted spoon and place in a bowl of warm water as you finish cooking the remaining eggs.

Toast the bread. Rub the garlic clove across the surface of the toast, then spread it with butter. Top with some of the spinach and an egg. Sprinkle the egg with salt, pepper, and parmesan. Serve warm.

Hedgehog Potatoes

2 lb (1 kg) small potatoes (Desiree, Patrone, Bison, or Yukon Gold), washed and dried

1 teaspoon flaked sea salt (or coarse sea salt pounded in a mortar and pestle until flaky)

1/2 teaspoon freshly ground black pepper

1/4 teaspoon cayenne pepper

1/2 cup (125 g) unsalted butter

PLANNING AHEAD: These potatoes can be half cooked several hours in advance and finished under the grill before serving.

Preheat the top grill of the oven. Oil a large baking sheet. Cut the potatoes in half lengthwise. Use a pastry cutter to press deep cross-hatched ridges into the cut side of the potatoes. If you do not have a pastry cutter, use a knife to cut the diagonal grooves. Put the potatoes on the baking tray cut side up. Sprinkle with the salt, pepper, and cayenne. Put a thin pad of butter on each potato.

Put the tray toward the top of the oven near the grill. Grill the potatoes until they are deep brown on top and easily pierced with a fork. If the potatoes threaten to burn under the grill and are not sufficiently tender inside, turn off the grill and bake in the middle of the oven at 400°F/200°C/ gas 6 until tender. Serve hot.

Creamy Apple Tart

PASTRY

1½ cups (225 g) all-purpose (plain) flour

¼ cup (50 g) superfine (caster) sugar

⅛ teaspoon salt

½ cup (125 g) cold unsalted butter, cut into chunks

1 egg + 1 egg yolk

FILLING

6 tart cooking apples (such as Granny Smith or
    Cox's Orange Pippins)

3 tablespoons lemon juice

½ cup (100 g) unsalted butter

½ cup (100 g) Vanilla Sugar (see page 140)

6 tablespoons Calvados or apple brandy

3 egg yolks + 1 egg

1 cup (250 ml) heavy (double) cream

1 teaspoon cinnamon

¼ teaspoon nutmeg

Heavy (double) cream, to serve

PLANNING AHEAD: The tart is good served warm the day it is made or cold the following day. It will keep for 4 days in the refrigerator.

PASTRY: In a large bowl, mix the flour, sugar, and salt. Cut in the butter with a pastry cutter or use your fingers until the mixture resembles coarse crumbs. Beat the egg and extra yolk together, then add to the mixture. Mix quickly with your fingers and form the dough into a disk. Wrap in waxed paper and refrigerate for 1 hour.

Roll the dough on a floured surface into a 14-inch (35-cm) circle, ⅛-inch (3 mm) thick. Line a 12-inch (30-cm) tart pan with the pastry. Crimp the edges in a decorative fashion. Refrigerate for 30 minutes to 1 hour.

Preheat the oven to 400°F/200°C/gas 6.

FILLING: Peel, core, and quarter the apples. Toss the apple quarters in a bowl with the lemon juice as you cut them. Melt the butter in a large skillet (frying pan) over medium-high heat. Add the apple pieces (but not any extra lemon juice from their soaking bowl) and toss to coat in the butter. Cook for 5 minutes, stirring occasionally. Add the sugar. Cook for 5 minutes more, shaking occasionally so that the sugar does not burn. At this point the sugar should be melted and beginning to caramelize, and the apples should be golden and softened (but not mushy and falling apart).

Add the Calvados, then light a match—stand back so you don't burn yourself—and flambée the alcohol. Gently shake the pan until the flames die down. Remove from the heat and let cool.

In a medium bowl, whisk together the egg yolks, egg, cream, cinnamon, and nutmeg. Place the cooled apple pieces in concentric circles on the pastry dough. Pour the custard over the apples. Bake for 35–40 minutes, or until the pastry is golden brown and the custard is golden and set. Cool on a rack for 20 minutes. Serve warm, at room temperature, or chilled with the cream.

English Garden Party

Lavender Lemonade
Tea
Cucumber Sandwiches
Mrs. S's Cheese Sablés
Fresh Pea Soup with Mint
Stilton and Chive Scones
Kedgeree
Baked Monkfish
Flower Salad
Summer Pudding

Wine Suggestions: a dry rosé, a sparkling wine,
or Mandarossa Grecanico from Settesoli

The stereotype that English food is bland and overcooked can be officially put to rest. The infusion of culinary ideas from other cultures (India, Italy, and North Africa are just three examples) and the return to traditional English cooking with local products and wild herbs has revitalized the cuisine.

I would especially like to thank Lizzie ("Wiz") Clift and Diana Singleton for showing me how delicious real English food can be. They have been generous in sharing their knowledge of wild foods and gardening and have taught me more than a thing or two in the kitchen.

Lavender Lemonade

¼ cup (10 g) English culinary lavender
(flowers only, no stems, leaves, or husks)
1 quart (1 liter) boiling water
1 cup (200 g) sugar
1¼ cups (310 ml) fresh lemon juice
2 blackberries (for color only; optional)

In a large teapot, seep the lavender flowers and a blackberry or two in the boiling water for 10 minutes. Strain the tea into a large pitcher. Add the sugar and stir to dissolve. Pour in the lemon juice and stir well. Chill the lemonade until ready to use. Serve in tall glasses over ice.

Tea

A good quality loose tea such as Darjeeling, Assam,
English Breakfast, or Keemun
Boiling water
A small pitcher of milk
A dish of honey
Sugar bowl
Lemon slices
A large teapot and a tea strainer

Rinse a large teapot with a splash of boiling water. Add a tablespoon or more of tea leaves, depending upon the type of tea you choose and how strong you like your tea. Fill the pot with boiling water. Seep for 3–5 minutes.

Strain the tea into individual cups. Serve hot with milk, honey, lemon, and sugar on the side.

Cucumber Sandwiches

12 thin slices whole-wheat, whole grain, or dark rye bread
1 recipe Herb Cream Cheese (see page 139)
2 English cucumbers, thinly sliced crosswise
Salt
1½ cups (200 g) watercress
4 tablespoons butter, softened
¼ cup (25 g) toasted sesame seeds
¼ cup (25 g) poppy seeds

PLANNING AHEAD: The sandwiches can be made an hour or two in advance.

Spread a layer of the Herb Cream Cheese on all the slices of bread. Layer six of the pieces of bread with cucumber slices, a pinch of salt, and some watercress. Top with the remaining slices of bread, pressing down firmly. Cut the crusts off the sandwiches. Cut each sandwich on the diagonal into four triangular pieces. Butter the short sides of the triangles. Dip one buttered edge into the sesame seeds and the other into the poppy seeds.

Arrange the sandwich triangles on a platter and serve with tea.

Mrs. S's Cheese Sablés

1⅔ cups (250 g) all-purpose (plain) flour

⅓ cup (50 g) semolina flour

2 cups (250 g) coarsely grated parmesan
    (or part parmesan and part sharp cheddar)

1 teaspoon mustard powder

½ teaspoon freshly ground black pepper

½ teaspoon salt

1 cup (250 g) cold unsalted butter

1 egg, lightly beaten

1 cup (125 g) extra finely grated parmesan, to sprinkle

This recipe comes from Diana Singleton of Colwall, Herefordshire. They are best cheesy biscuits I have ever eaten. Once you start eating them it's hard to stop, and they are a perfect snack to accompany sparkling wine or soup.

PLANNING AHEAD: The sablés keep for one week in an airtight container.

In a large mixing bowl, combine the dry ingredients and mix well with a fork. Cut in the butter and work through with your fingers until the mixture resembles coarse crumbs. Alternatively, pulse all the ingredients, except the egg and extra parmesan, in a food processor until the mixture forms small balls. Knead the dough briefly and divide it into four small disks. The dough should be crumbly and barely hold together. Wrap the disks in waxed paper and refrigerate for 1 hour.

Preheat the oven to 375°F/190°C/gas 5. Line two large baking sheets with waxed paper.

Roll the dough in batches, keeping the remaining dough refrigerated. On a floured surface, roll a disk into a large, thin rectangle, about ⅛ inch (3 mm) thick. Brush with the egg and sprinkle with a good coat of finely grated parmesan. Cut the rectangle into long 2-inch (5-cm) wide strips. Cut each strip on the diagonal into small triangular pieces. Transfer the sablés to a prepared baking sheet with a spatula, spacing well so that they are not touching. Refrigerate for 15 minutes before baking. Roll out another batch of sablés while the first sheet is in the refrigerator.

Bake for 12–15 minutes, or until golden brown. Cool on a wire rack. Serve at room temperature.

Fresh Pea Soup with Mint

2 tablespoons butter

1 cup (250 ml) chopped green onions (spring onions)

2 tablespoons finely chopped Italian flat-leaf parsley

1 quart (1 liter) chicken-flavored Quick Stock (see page 138)

1 tablespoon fresh thyme leaves

½ teaspoon salt

5 cups (750 g) fresh or frozen baby peas

6 tablespoons heavy (double) cream

Freshly ground black pepper to taste

A handful of fresh mint leaves, torn

Crème fraîche or sour cream, to garnish

Edible flower (nasturtium or pansy), to garnish (optional)

PLANNING AHEAD: The soup can be made a day in advance.

In a large soup pot, melt the butter over moderately low heat. Add the green onions and parsley and sauté gently for 2 minutes. Do not let the onion brown. Add the chicken stock, thyme, and salt. Bring to a boil. Add the peas and simmer until they are tender. Blend the soup in batches (be careful when blending hot liquids). Return to the pot. Stir in the cream. Taste for pepper.

Serve hot. Garnish each serving with a spoonful of crème fraîche or sour cream and the fresh mint leaves. An edible flower, such as a nasturtium or pansy, looks pretty as a garnish.

Stilton and Chive Scones

1½ cups (225 g) stone-ground white flour

1 tablespoon baking powder

1 teaspoon mustard powder

Dash of cayenne pepper

Pinch of salt

⅛ teaspoon freshly ground black pepper

3 tablespoons cold unsalted butter

3 oz (90 g) Stilton cheese, broken into pea-sized crumbles
    (or ½ cup (60 g) grated sharp cheddar
    and 1 oz (30 g) crumbled blue cheese)

1 tablespoon minced fresh thyme

1 tablespoon minced fresh chives

½ cup (125 ml) milk

1 egg yolk

⅓ cup (40 g) grated sharp cheddar cheese

PLANNING AHEAD: The scones are best warm, but they are also good toasted the next day.

In a large mixing bowl, combine the flour, baking powder, mustard, cayenne, salt, and pepper. Cut in the butter until it is in pea-sized pieces. Add the Stilton, thyme, and chives and mix well. Pour in the milk and stir. Knead the dough briefly to combine. It should be fairly soft and sticky. If it is too crumbly, add a bit more milk.

On a floured surface, roll or pat the dough until it is ¾-inch (2-cm) thick. Use a 2-inch (5-cm) circular cookie cutter to cut out the scones. Place on a lightly buttered baking sheet, with space between each scone. Brush the tops with egg yolk, and then sprinkle with the cheddar. Chill for 20 minutes in the refrigerator.

Preheat the oven to 400°F/200°C/gas 6.

Bake the scones for 15–18 minutes, or until they are puffed and golden brown on top. Cool for 5–10 minutes on a wire rack. Serve warm with butter.

Kedgeree

3 cups (600 g) long-grain white rice

30 saffron threads

2 cups (500 ml) heavy (double) cream

1 teaspoon ground turmeric

¼–½ teaspoon cayenne (depending upon how spicy
    you like it)

¾ teaspoon salt

2 teaspoons pink peppercorns, crushed in a mortar

1 lb (500 g) smoked mackerel, haddock or trout,
    coarsely chopped

4 hard-boiled eggs, peeled and chopped

6 small green onions (spring onions), white and pale green
    parts only, finely sliced

2 large handfuls fresh cilantro (coriander) leaves, to garnish

An English brunch classic of Indian origins: saffron rice with fish and spices.
PLANNING AHEAD: The rice can be cooked in advance.

In a medium saucepan, bring the rice and 3 cups (750 ml) of water to a boil. Add the saffron, cover, and reduce the heat to very low. Cook until the rice is tender and fluffy, about 20 minutes.

In a small saucepan over medium heat, bring the cream with the turmeric, cayenne, salt, and pink pepper to a boil. Reduce the heat and simmer for 2 minutes. Remove from the heat.

In a large bowl, mix the cooked saffron rice with the smoked fish, egg, and the green onions. Stir in the cream with the spices. Taste for salt and seasoning.

Butter two 1½-quart (1.5 liter) soufflé molds or other deep-sided dishes or bowls. Divide the rice mixture evenly between the two molds. Press it firmly into each dish, and then unmold onto serving plates. Decorate with the fresh cilantro. Serve warm.

Baked Monkfish

3 lb (1.5 kg) monkfish tails, skinned and cut crosswise
    into 2-inch (5-cm) thick medallions

2 tablespoons extra-virgin olive oil

2 red onions, sliced

$\frac{1}{4}$ teaspoon salt

5 cloves garlic, minced

2 tablespoons fresh rosemary

$\frac{1}{2}$ cup (125 ml) dry white wine

2 tablespoons heavy (double) cream

Freshly ground black pepper to taste

2 cups (500 g) ripe cherry tomatoes

2 tablespoons butter

Preheat the oven to 350°F/180°/gas 4. Lightly butter a large baking dish.

In a large skillet (frying pan), warm the olive oil over medium heat. Add the onion and salt and sauté gently until the onion is soft, about 10 minutes. Add the garlic and rosemary. Sauté for 30 seconds. Do not let the garlic brown. Pour in the wine and simmer for 2 minutes. Remove from the heat. Add the cream and fresh black pepper to taste.

Toss the pieces of monkfish in the onion mixture to coat them thoroughly. Use a spatula to scrape all the ingredients in the skillet into the baking dish. Distribute the fish evenly in the baking dish. Place the tomatoes around the fish. Top the fish with small pads of butter. Cover with foil and bake for 20–25 minutes, or until the fish is white and tender when pierced with a fork. Taste for salt and seasoning.

Serve hot or at room temperature.

Flower Salad

12 cups (300 g) mixed baby lettuce

3–4 cups (100 g) mixed edible flowers (nasturtium, borage,
    pansy, rose petals, violets, periwinkle, or fennel flowers)

1 recipe Glazed Walnuts (see recipe Mixed Baby Greens with
    Pears and Blue Cheese, page 54)

DRESSING

1 tablespoon finely chopped shallot

1 tablespoon red wine vinegar

$\frac{1}{2}$ teaspoon salt

$\frac{1}{4}$ teaspoon freshly ground black pepper

$\frac{1}{2}$ teaspoon sugar

4 tablespoons extra-virgin olive oil

1 teaspoon finely chopped chives

12 fresh basil leaves, finely chopped

Wash and spin dry all the lettuces. Tear into small pieces and put in a large salad bowl. Soak the flowers in a basin or large bowl of water to remove any insects. Drain on paper towels.

DRESSING: Whisk all the ingredients to together. Taste for seasoning.

Pour the dressing over the lettuces and toss well. Top with the glazed walnuts and the flowers. Serve.

Flower Salad and **Baked Monkfish**

Summer Pudding

2 lb (1 kg) fresh or thawed frozen berries
   (raspberries, blackberries, red currants,
   black currants, blueberries, or wild strawberries)

1 cup (200 g) sugar

2 tablespoons Cassis liqueur

1 tablespoon finely grated lemon zest

2 tablespoons fresh lemon juice

1/2 loaf sliced white bread, crusts cut off

1/2 cup (125 ml) heavy (double) cream

4 tablespoons plain low-fat yogurt

4 tablespoons crème fraîche

PLANNING AHEAD: This summer pudding needs to be made a day in advance and refrigerated overnight.

In a large saucepan, combine the berries with the sugar, Cassis, lemon zest, and lemon juice. Heat for about 2 minutes, or just long enough to dissolve the sugar but not to cook the berries. Cool to room temperature.

Use a large soufflé dish or deep bowl. Line with the bread. Make sure there are no gaps and the bread is completely covering the surface. Spoon in the berry mixture. Hold back some of the juices to use later. Cover the top of the berries with more bread. Cover with plastic wrap, and then weigh down with a plate that fits into the soufflé dish or bowl. Put a couple of heavy cans of food on top of the plate to compress the pudding. Refrigerate overnight.

Put a large serving platter, with a slight rim to hold in the juices, over the top of the soufflé dish. Invert to unmold the summer pudding. Pour the reserved juices over any part of the pudding that is still white.

In a medium mixing bowl, beat the cream until it forms firm peaks. Fold in the yogurt and crème fraîche. Serve the summer pudding with the whipped cream mixture.

Southern States

Lemon Verbena Iced Tea
Melon Salad
Buttermilk Biscuits
Eggs in Ham Cups
Cheesy Green Onion Grits
Pork Chops
Sue Ellen's Fried Green Tomatoes
Skillet Corn Bread
Black-Eyed Peas
Collard Greens with Bacon and Onion
Peach Blackberry Crisp with Vanilla Ice Cream

No brunch book would be complete without a proper Southern meal.
Southerners are famous for their hospitality and know exactly how to spend
a leisurely summer Sunday with friends.

This menu is inspired by my dear friend Sue Ellen, a fabulous cook,
who took me in hand when I was 11 and began to teach me how to make a few things
in the kitchen. Much of my love of food and cooking comes from her. Sue Ellen grew up
in Oklahoma, and these recipes are variations on some of the dishes her grandmother,
mother, and aunts would prepare for Sunday "dinner" after church.

Lemon Verbena Iced Tea

1 oz (30 g) dried lemon verbena leaves
1¼ quarts (1.25 liters) boiling water
Ice
Lemon wedges and fresh sprigs of lemon verbena, to garnish

PLANNING AHEAD: The tea can be made a day or two in advance and stored in the refrigerator.

In a large teapot or heatproof jug, seep the lemon verbena leaves and boiling water for 15 minutes. Strain. Let the tea come to room temperature. Serve in tall glasses over ice with garnishes.

Melon Salad

½ small watermelon
1 cantaloupe (rock melon)
1 honeydew melon
Sprigs of mint, to garnish

PLANNING AHEAD: The salad can be made the night before. Cover and refrigerate until ready to serve.

Cut the cantaloupe and honeydew in half and remove the seeds. Use a melon baller to scoop out the flesh of all the melons, or use a knife to cut the fruit into bite-sized pieces. Put the melon balls in a serving bowl. Refrigerate until ready to serve. Garnish with mint.

Buttermilk Biscuits

1 cup (150 g) cake flour
1 cup (150 g) all-purpose (plain) flour
1 tablespoon baking powder
½ teaspoon salt
½ teaspoon baking soda (bicarbonate of soda)
½ cup (125 g) cold unsalted butter, cut into small chunks
⅔ cup (150 ml) buttermilk (or milk with 1 teaspoon
    white vinegar)

HONEY BUTTER
Honey
Butter

PLANNING AHEAD: These are best warm from the oven, but they are also good split open and toasted the next day. The biscuits can also be formed in advance and refrigerated on the baking sheet until ready to pop in the hot oven.

Preheat the oven to 450°F/230°C/gas 8.

In a large mixing bowl, sift together the flours, baking powder, salt, and baking soda. Cut in the butter with a pastry cutter and then mix with your fingers until the mixture resembles coarse crumbs. Stir the flour mixture with a fork as you pour in the buttermilk. Knead the dough very briefly to integrate. Roll the dough on a floured surface until it is ½-inch (1-cm) thick. Cut out the biscuits with a 2-inch (5-cm) round cookie cutter. Place the biscuits on an ungreased baking sheet. Bake for 10–12 minutes, until risen and golden brown on top. Transfer the hot biscuits to a cooling rack. Serve warm with honey butter.

HONEY BUTTER: Simply mix equal parts honey and butter together until creamy. Serve in a dish alongside the biscuits. Honey butter is also good on the skillet corn bread (see page 80).

Lemon Verbena Iced Tea and Melon Salad with Buttermilk Biscuits

Eggs in Ham Cups

¹/₄ cup (60 g) finely chopped shallots

1 tablespoon butter

1 tablespoon finely chopped parsley

1 tablespoon dry vermouth

2 tablespoons sour cream

Dash of cayenne pepper

¹/₄ teaspoon freshly ground black pepper

6 slices of cured ham without holes (Virginia ham,
    Prosciutto di Parma, or Black Forest)

6 eggs

Salt and freshly ground black pepper to taste

Preheat the oven to 400°F/200°C/gas 6.

In a small skillet (frying pan), sauté the shallots with the butter over moderately low heat. Do not let the shallots brown. When they are soft, add the parsley and vermouth. Cook for 1 minute more over medium heat. Remove from the heat. Stir in the sour cream, cayenne, and pepper.

Line a 6-cup muffin tray with a slice of ham. The ham should stick up above the rim of the muffin cup. Make sure there are no holes in the ham lining. Spoon the shallot mixture into the bottoms of the cups. Crack an egg into each cup.

Bake for 15 minutes, until the egg whites are cooked and the yolks are still runny. Serve hot.

Cheesy Green Onion Grits

1¹/₄ quarts (1.25 liters) water

¹/₄ teaspoon salt

1 cup (150 g) grits (not instant)

5 green onions (spring onions), white and pale green parts
    only finely chopped

2 cups (250 g) grated white cheese (white cheddar, provolone
    piccante, or medium-aged pecorino)

Finely chopped green onions (spring onions), to garnish

In a large saucepan, bring the water and salt to a boil over moderately high heat. Stir in the grits. Reduce the heat to a simmer, cover, and cook for 10 minutes. Stir occasionally. Add the green onions. Cover and continue cooking for 10 more minutes. Stir in the cheese. When the cheese has melted, remove from the heat and serve immediately. Garnish with the chopped green onions.

Cheesy Green Onion Grits and **Eggs in Ham Cups**

Pork Chops

6 pork chops

4 cloves garlic

$^3/_4$ teaspoon coarse sea salt

$^1/_2$ teaspoon whole peppercorns

2 tablespoons fresh rosemary

2 tablespoons extra-virgin olive oil

Lemon wedges, for garnish

PLANNING AHEAD: The pork chops are best if marinated overnight. They are also excellent barbecued.

Wash the chops and pat dry with paper towels. Use kitchen scissors to snip radiating cuts (about one every inch or 2.5 cm) in any fat surrounding the chop; this prevents the chop from buckling during cooking.

In a mortar, crush the garlic with the salt and pepper into a paste. Add the rosemary and oil and mix well. Put the chops in a single layer in large shallow dish. Rub the garlic and rosemary mixture all over both sides of the chops. Cover and marinate for 2 hours, or overnight in the refrigerator.

Bring to room temperature before cooking.

Place a large skillet (frying pan) over moderately high heat. Add the pork chops. Brown the chops on both sides (about 3–4 minutes per side). Cook the chops until they are white with only the tiniest hint of pink when you cut into the very center, or to your preferred level of doneness. Garnish with the lemon wedges.

Sue Ellen's Fried Green Tomatoes

I cup (150 g) cornmeal

$^1/_2$ cup (75 g) all-purpose (plain) flour

I tablespoon sugar

$^1/_4$ teaspoon freshly ground black pepper

Pinch of cayenne pepper

2 lb (I kg) green tomatoes, cut into $^1/_2$-inch (1-cm) thick crosswise slices

$^1/_2$ cup (125 ml) buttermilk (or milk plus I teaspoon vinegar)

Salt to taste

Vegetable oil or bacon grease, for frying (bacon dripping is traditional, but canola or peanut oil works fine)

PLANNING AHEAD: The tomatoes are best hot from the pan. However, they can be made 30 minutes in advance and kept warm on a baking sheet in the oven.

In a shallow bowl, mix the cornmeal, flour, sugar, pepper, and cayenne. Dip the tomato slices in the buttermilk, then coat well with the cornmeal mixture. Press the slices into the cornmeal to make a good coating. Pour a $^1/_2$-inch (1-cm) layer of the oil of your choice into a large, heavy (preferably cast-iron) skillet (frying pan).

Place the oil over moderately high heat until almost smoking. Add the tomatoes a few at a time without crowding. Fry until they are golden brown on the bottom. Reduce the heat to medium if the tomatoes threaten to burn. Turn them gently with a spatula and brown the other side. When the tomatoes are deep golden brown on both sides, remove from the pan and drain on paper towels. Repeat until all the tomatoes are cooked. Sprinkle with salt. Serve hot.

Pork Chops and Sue Ellen's Fried Green Tomatoes

Skillet Corn Bread

1 tablespoon butter, for the skillet

1 cup (150 g) all-purpose (plain) flour

1 cup (150 g) cornmeal

1 tablespoon sugar

1 tablespoon baking powder

1/2 teaspoon salt

2 eggs, lightly beaten

1 cup (250 ml) milk

4 tablespoons melted butter or vegetable oil

3/4 cup (120 g) fresh corn kernels (or canned corn, drained)

PLANNING AHEAD: The corn bread is best the day it is made, but it is also good reheated. It lasts for 2–3 days wrapped in foil.

Preheat the oven to 400°F/200°C/gas 6.

Put a 9 (23-cm) or 10-inch (25-cm) cast-iron skillet with at least 2-inch (5-cm) high sides in the oven with the tablespoon of butter. In a large bowl, combine all the dry ingredients. Stir well with a fork. In a separate bowl, combine the eggs, milk, melted butter, and corn. Make a well in the dry mixture, then pour the wet ingredients in all at once. Stir briefly with a spatula to combine.

Remove the hot skillet from the oven and swirl to coat the entire pan in the melted butter. Pour in the batter. Bake for 20–25 minutes, or until golden and a toothpick inserted in the center comes out clean. Serve the corn bread hot from the skillet.

Black-Eyed Peas (Cow Peas)

2 cups (400 g) dried black-eyed peas

3 cloves garlic, cracked with the flat side of a knife and peeled

1 onion, diced

1 bay leaf

1 teaspoon coarse sea salt

1 teaspoon whole black peppercorns, coarsely crushed in a mortar

Pinch of red pepper flakes

1 oz (30 g) thick chunk of smoked bacon or a small ham hock

1 sprig fresh sage

PLANNING AHEAD: The dry black-eyed peas need to soak overnight. When cooked, they will last for several days in the refrigerator.

Rinse the black-eyed peas. Put them in a large bowl and cover with plenty of cold water. There should be at least 2 inches (5 cm) of water covering the peas. Add more water as needed as it is absorbed. Soak overnight.

Drain the peas in a colander. Place in a large pot with remaining ingredients. Cover with fresh water. Bring to a boil over medium heat. Reduce to low. Simmer, partially covered, for 1 1/2 hours, or until the peas are tender but not falling apart. Stir occasionally during cooking and check that there is enough water (add more if needed). Remove the sprig of sage and bay leaf. Reserve the piece of bacon for another use. Serve hot.

Collard Greens with Bacon and Onion

3 lb (1.5 kg) collard or mustard greens, washed, stems and ribs removed, coarsely chopped

3 1/2 oz (100 g) sliced bacon, chopped

1 large onion, chopped

1/8 teaspoon red pepper flakes

4 tablespoons dry vermouth

3 cups (750 ml) water

1 tablespoon cider vinegar

2 tablespoons brown sugar

Salt and freshly ground black pepper to taste

PLANNING AHEAD: The collard greens can be made a day in advance and reheated.

In a large heavy pot, cook the bacon over medium heat. When the bacon is crisp and brown, add the onion and red pepper. Sauté until the onion is soft, but do not brown. Pour in the vermouth and let it bubble and evaporate. Add the water, cider vinegar and brown sugar. Stir to dissolve the sugar. Bring the mixture to a boil. Add the collard greens in batches as it wilts down. Cover and simmer for 1 hour, or until the greens are very tender. Stir occasionally. Taste for salt and pepper. Serve hot with the skillet corn bread (see recipe above) to sop up the "pot liquor" (the broth at the bottom of the pot).

Black-Eyed Peas, Collard Greens with Bacon and Onion, and Skillet Corn Bread

Peach Blackberry Crisp

6 large ripe peaches, peeled, pitted, and sliced

3 cups (750 g) fresh blackberries

1/3 cup (70 g) Vanilla Sugar (see page 140)

Juice of 1/2 lemon

CRUMBLE TOPPING

1/2 cup (50 g) rolled oats

8 amaretti cookies, crushed

1/2 cup (100 g) firmly packed brown sugar

3/4 cup (125 g) all-purpose (plain) flour

1/4 teaspoon salt

1/2 teaspoon cinnamon

7 tablespoons cold unsalted butter, cut into chunks

This crisp is also excellent when made with pears, cherries, plums, apricots, nectarines, apples, or whatever fruit is to hand. I mix and match fruit depending upon what is in season. If the peaches are difficult to peel, plunge them into boiling water for 1 minute, then rinse in cold water. The skins will slip off easily.

PLANNING AHEAD: This crisp is quick and easy to make, but it's also good reheated the next day.

Preheat the oven to 375°F/190°C/gas 5.

CRUMBLE TOPPING: Put all the ingredients, except the butter, in a food processor and pulse until well combined. Add the butter and pulse until the mixture looks like coarse crumbs. To make by hand: chop the oats until they are half their original size (or use quick oats). Mix with the crushed amaretti, brown sugar, flour, salt, and cinnamon. Cut in the butter and mix with your fingers until the mixture resembles coarse crumbs.

Butter a 2-quart (2-liter) baking dish. In a large bowl, toss the peach slices and the blackberries with the sugar and lemon juice. Spoon the fruit mixture into the dish. Cover with the crumble topping.

Bake for 40–45 minutes, or until the fruit is bubbling and the topping is crisp and brown. Serve warm with vanilla ice cream.

Vanilla Ice Cream

1 vanilla bean pod

1/2 cup (100 g) + 2 tablespoons superfine (caster) sugar

2 egg yolks

1 teaspoon vanilla extract (essence)

1 1/2 cups (375 ml) whole milk

1 1/4 cups (310 ml) heavy (double) cream

PLANNING AHEAD: Make the ice cream the day before. It lasts for up to a month in the freezer.

Split the vanilla bean in half lengthwise and scrap the tiny black vanilla beans into the superfine sugar. In a large bowl, beat the sugar with the egg yolks and vanilla extract until pale and creamy. Gradually pour in the milk and stir until well mixed. In a separate bowl, beat the cream into soft peaks. Fold the whipped cream into the egg and cream mixture until well combined but still light.

Pour the ice cream mixture into an ice cream machine and follow manufacturer's instructions. If you do not have an ice cream maker, transfer the ice cream to an airtight container and put in the freezer. Stir the ice cream every couple of hours until it reaches the desired consistency (about 4–6 hours in the freezer).

Peach Blackberry Crisp with **Vanilla Ice Cream**

Ski Lodge

Mocha
Stacey's Banana Muffins
Rosemary Almond Waffles
High C Salad with Mint Syrup
Scrambled Eggs
Spicy Peppered Bacon
Baked Apples with Amaretti Stuffing
Mulled Wine
Rice Pudding
Plum Compote

One of the many joys of spending time in the snow is that you can eat almost anything you want and still burn off all the calories skiing, hiking, sledding, and playing. The combination of cold air and exercise makes for huge appetites, and the body craves something warm and satisfying.

In college, a good friend had a family cabin on Lake Tahoe. A group of us would go up in the winter to cross-country ski. We would ski in the morning, go back to the cabin for a long brunch, and then go back out in the snow again. So whether you are in a cabin in the snow, or simply live in a cold climate and want to spend a snug Sunday at home with friends, this brunch menu comes with plenty of internal heating.

Mocha

1 quart (1 liter) milk

4 tablespoons good quality unsweetened cocoa

3 tablespoons Vanilla Sugar (see page 140)

1 cup (250 ml) very strong coffee, or 4–5 shots of espresso

Whipped cream (optional)

In a heavy saucepan, heat the milk, cocoa, and vanilla sugar. Beat with a wire whisk as it cooks to thoroughly mix and remove any lumps. Heat the mixture until almost boiling. Remove from the heat. Pour in the hot coffee or espresso and stir. Serve hot in mugs with whipped cream, if desired.

Stacey's Banana Muffins

1 cup (150 g) unbleached all-purpose (plain) flour

1 cup (150 g) whole-wheat (wholemeal) flour

1 teaspoon baking soda (bicarbonate of soda)

1 teaspoon ground cinnamon

1/2 teaspoon ground cardamom

1/4 teaspoon nutmeg

1/2 cup (125 g) butter, at room temperature

1/2 cup (100 g) firmly packed brown sugar

1/2 cup (100 g) sugar

2 large eggs

3 large overripe bananas, mashed,
   weighing about 1 1/2 cups (375 g) mashed

1 teaspoon vanilla extract (essence)

1/2 cup (125 ml) buttermilk (or 4 tablespoons plain yogurt
   and 4 tablespoons milk)

1/2 cup (75 g) chopped, toasted walnuts

Don't skip the whole-wheat flour or the cardamom in this recipe as they make all the difference.

PLANNING AHEAD: These muffins stay moist and delicious for 4 days in an airtight container.

Preheat the oven to 375°F/190°C/gas 5. Butter a 12-cup muffin tray.

In a medium bowl, combine the flours, baking soda, and spices. In a large bowl, beat the butter and sugars at medium-high speed until pale and fluffy. At medium speed beat in the eggs one at a time until just combined. Add the mashed banana and vanilla. Reduce the mixing speed to low. Add the dry ingredients with the buttermilk and mix until well combined. Fold in the walnuts.

Fill the muffin cups three-quarters full. Bake for 18–20 minutes, or until the muffins are golden brown, springy to the touch, and a toothpick inserted in the center comes out clean. Cool on a rack for 10 minutes. Serve warm or at room temperature.

Rosemary Almond Waffles

1 cup (150 g) all-purpose (plain) flour

1/2 cup (75 g) whole-wheat (wholemeal) flour

1/4 cup (30 g) rye flour

2 teaspoons baking powder

1/4 teaspoon baking soda (bicarbonate of soda)

1/2 teaspoon salt

1 tablespoon sugar

1 1/2 cups (375 ml) whole milk

2 tablespoons fresh lemon juice

3/4 cup (180 g) unsalted butter, melted, plus 2 tablespoons more for the waffle iron

3 eggs, lightly beaten

2 tablespoons finely chopped fresh rosemary

1 tablespoon finely grated orange zest

1/2 cup (75 g) almonds, toasted and finely chopped

Real maple syrup or honey, to serve

Follow the instructions for your particular waffle iron to get the desired level of doneness. Do not lift the iron while steam is still emerging.

In a large bowl, combine the flours, baking powder, baking soda, salt, and sugar. In a small bowl, combine the milk and lemon juice and let stand for 5 minutes. Add the melted butter, eggs, rosemary, and orange zest to the milk. Make a well in the flour mixture and pour the milk mixture in all at once. Stir with a spatula until mixed. The batter will be slightly lumpy. Fold in the almonds.

Brush the waffle iron with melted butter. These waffles are best toasted to a deep golden brown, about 5 minutes on high heat for many waffle irons. For a 6-inch (15-cm) regular (not Belgian) waffle grill, use approximately 1/2 cup (125 ml) batter per waffle. Brush the iron with more butter, if needed, before pouring batter for the next waffle.

Keep the cooked waffles on a baking tray in a warm oven until ready to serve. Serve with warm maple syrup or honey.

High C Salad with Mint Syrup

MINT SYRUP

3/4 cup (180 ml) water

4 tablespoons dry white wine

1/2 cup (100 g) sugar

1 cup (250 ml) fresh mint leaves

SALAD

3 navel oranges

2 blood oranges

1 pink grapefruit

1 yellow grapefruit

1 sugar loaf pineapple, or 1/2 a regular pineapple

1 large ripe mango

2 kiwis

Sprigs of fresh mint, to garnish

This refreshing fruit salad is high in vitamin C to help fight winter colds.

PLANNING AHEAD: The mint syrup can be made up to a week in advance.

MINT SYRUP: Pour the water, wine, and sugar into a heavy saucepan. Stir over medium heat until the sugar has dissolved. Add the mint and bring to a boil. Reduce heat to low and cook until the syrup has reduced by half, about 15 minutes. Remove from heat. Strain and set aside to cool.

SALAD: Slice off the very top and bottom of the oranges and grapefruits. Peel and cut away the outer white pith with a sharp knife. Over a bowl, cut each segment of the citrus away from its membranes and seeds. Catch the cutting juice in the bowl. Cut the top and bottom off the pineapple. Cut away the skin. Quarter the pineapple and remove the tough central core. Slice into bite-sized sections.

Cut the two meaty halves of the mango off its pit. Cut a grid pattern, almost to the skin, on each half. Pop the skin upward so the cubes of mango are exposed like a porcupine's back. Cut the cubes of mango off the skin.

Peel the kiwi. Cut in half lengthwise and then slice crosswise to make half-moon pieces.

Put all the fruit in a serving bowl. Pour the reserved citrus juices on top of the fruit. Drizzle spoonfuls of mint syrup over the fruit to taste. Garnish with the sprigs of mint and serve.

Rosemary Almond Waffles and **High C Salad with Mint Syrup**

Scrambled Eggs

8 eggs

4 tablespoons cream

2 tablespoons whole milk

2 tablespoons finely sliced green onions (spring onions),
pale green and green part only

2 tablespoons butter

Salt and freshly ground black pepper to taste

Dash of cayenne pepper (optional)

PLANNING AHEAD: These eggs take only minutes to prepare and cook. They are best made at the last minute and served immediately.

In a large bowl, beat the eggs with a fork or wire whisk just long enough to blend the yolks and whites. Add the cream, milk, green onions, salt, pepper, and cayenne (if using) and mix to blend. Melt the butter in a large nonstick skillet (frying pan) over medium heat. Pour the egg mixture into the hot pan. Let the eggs set for 30 seconds and then stir and fold with a rubber spatula until the eggs have thickened to almost the desired consistency. Do not overcook the eggs as they will continue to thicken off the heat. Serve immediately.

Spicy Peppered Bacon

1 tablespoon black peppercorns

1/4–1/2 teaspoon dried Chipotle chile pepper flakes
(depending upon how spicy you like it)

1/4 teaspoon mustard powder

2 tablespoons firmly packed brown sugar

12 slices smoked bacon, weighing about 1 lb (500 g)

Chipotle chiles are jalapeño peppers that have been smoked and dried. They are used frequently in Mexican and Southwest cuisine (New Mexico, Texas) for their fiery, smoky flavor. If they are not available, use regular chile pepper flakes.

Preheat the oven to 350°F/180°C/gas 4.

Put a steel-wire cooling rack on a large baking tray. Arrange the slices of bacon on the rack (the bacon will be suspended above the baking tray, and most of the fat will drip onto the tray as it cooks). Crush the peppercorns in a mortar until they are coarsely ground.

In a small bowl, stir the pepper, Chipotle, dry mustard, and brown sugar until well mixed. Spoon approximately 1 teaspoon of the pepper mixture onto each slice of bacon. Use the back of the spoon to smooth the mixture across the entire surface of the bacon.

Put the bacon in the oven and bake for 20–25 minutes, depending upon how crisp you like it. Drain the bacon on paper towels (pepper-side up). Serve warm.

Scrambled Eggs with **Spicy Peppered Bacon**

Baked Apples with Amaretti Stuffing

6 firm, greenish Golden Delicious apples

1 cup (125 g) crushed amaretti biscuits

4 tablespoons unsalted butter, melted

1/2 teaspoon cinnamon

1/8 teaspoon nutmeg

1/4 teaspoon salt

1/8 teaspoon freshly ground black pepper

1/8 teaspoon allspice

1 teaspoon finely grated lemon zest

2 tablespoons finely chopped dried, sweetened cranberries

1 tablespoon dried currants

1 tablespoon pine nuts

3 tablespoons finely chopped nuts (almonds, pecans, pistachios, hazelnuts, or walnuts)

2 tablespoons fresh lemon juice

4 tablespoons Calvados, apple brandy, or dark rum

4 tablespoons apple juice

Plain yogurt, to garnish

PLANNING AHEAD: The stuffing for the apples can be made a day in advance and stored in an airtight container in the refrigerator. Bring to room temperature before using.

Preheat the oven to 350°F/180°C/gas 4. Butter an 11 x 7-inch (28 x 18-cm) baking dish with 2-inch (5-cm) deep sides.

Rinse the apples and pat dry. Peel the top quarter of each apple. Use a melon baller to scoop out the core and seeds to create a cavity. Be sure to remove all the tough fibers around the core, but leave the bottom of the apple intact. Brush the tops and insides of the apples with the lemon juice to prevent discoloring.

In a medium bowl, combine the amaretti crumbs, 2 tablespoons of the melted butter (reserve the remaining two for later), cinnamon, nutmeg, salt, pepper, allspice, cranberries, lemon zest, currants, and nuts. Mix well with a fork. Pack the stuffing into the apples. Put the stuffed apples into the baking dish.

Combine the Calvados, apple juice, and remaining 2 tablespoons of melted butter. Brush the outside of the apples with the mixture, and pour the remaining liquid on the bottom of the baking dish.

Bake uncovered for 35–40 minutes, basting the apples occasionally. The apples are done when they give little resistance when pierced with a sharp knife, but are not mushy and falling apart.

Serve the apples warm with their cooking juices and a spoonful of plain yogurt.

Mulled Wine

1 1/2 quarts (1.5 liters) young, dry red wine

1 stick cinnamon

3 cardamom pods

Zest of 1 lemon, preferably organic, cut in wide strips

Zest of 1 orange, preferably organic, cut in wide strips

3 whole cloves

1 teaspoon whole black peppercorns

1 bay leaf

Vanilla Sugar (see page 140), to taste

PLANNING AHEAD: The wine can be mulled the day before and reheated before serving.

Put the cinnamon, cardamom, lemon and orange zest, cloves, black pepper, and bay leaf on a piece of clean cheesecloth (muslin) and tie into a bundle. Pour the wine into a large heavy saucepan, add the spice sack, and bring to a boil. Reduce heat to low and simmer, partially covered, for 30 minutes to 1 hour.

Taste for sweetness. Add vanilla sugar to taste. Cook for 10 minutes more, stirring frequently to completely dissolve the sugar.

Serve hot in thick glass cups.

Rice Pudding

1¼ cups (250 ml) long-grain white rice

1½ cups (375 ml) water

½ teaspoon salt

⅓ cup (50 g) golden raisins (sultanas)

2 tablespoons dark rum

1¼ quarts (1.25 liters) whole milk

⅓ cup (70 g) Vanilla Sugar (see page 140)

1 teaspoon cinnamon

¼ teaspoon nutmeg

2 eggs, lightly beaten

½ cup (125 ml) whipping cream

½ cup (50 g) pistachios, lightly toasted and coarsely chopped

1 recipe of Plum Compote (recipe follows)

This rich, creamy pudding is offset by the slight sharpness of the plum compote.

PLANNING AHEAD: Make the rice pudding the day before and refrigerate overnight. Before serving, fold in the whipped cream, layer with the plum compote and top with the pistachios.

In a large heavy saucepan, bring the rice, water, and salt to a boil. Reduce to a simmer, cover and cook until the water is absorbed (about 10 minutes). Soak the raisins in the rum while the rice is cooking.

Pour the milk into the saucepan with the half-cooked rice. Add the vanilla sugar, cinnamon, and nutmeg. Bring to a boil and reduce to a simmer. Add the raisins and the rum they were soaking in. Cook, stirring frequently, for about 30 minutes, or until the pudding is thick and creamy like porridge. Do not overcook the pudding, or it will be solid instead of creamy when cool.

Ladle 1 cup (250 ml) of the hot pudding into the beaten eggs. Stir well. Add one more ladleful and stir again. Return the pudding with the beaten eggs to the saucepan and cook on very low heat for 1 minute (do not overcook the eggs or they will curdle and make the pudding grainy). Remove from the heat.

Cover the pudding to prevent a skin forming on top. Cool and then refrigerate overnight (or for at least 4 hours). Before serving, whip the cream and fold into the pudding. Use individual sundae or ice cream glasses. Put some plum compote in each glass, cover with a layer of rice pudding, then more plum compote, and a final layer of rice pudding. Top with the pistachios.

Plum Compote

2 lb (1 kg) ripe Italian Prune or Victoria plums, cut in half and pits removed

Juice of 1 lemon

¼ cup (50 g) Vanilla Sugar (see page 140)

PLANNING AHEAD: The plums can be cooked up to 5 days in advance. Cover and store in the refrigerator.

Preheat the oven to 350°F/180°C/gas 4. Butter a large casserole dish. Put the plum halves in the dish. Squeeze the lemon over the plums and sprinkle with the sugar. Bake for 30–40 minutes, or until the plums are soft and bubbly. Cool to room temperature. Serve with the rice pudding.

Rice Pudding with Plum Compote

Mexican

Horchata
Spicy Fruit Spears
Pico de Gallo Salsa
Guacamole
Ceviche Tostadas
Huevos Rancheros
Spanish Rice
Jalapeño Corn Muffins
Frijoles de la Olla
Chile Relleños
Blood Orange Flan
Mexican Coffee
Aztec Brownies

Serve with Mexican beer

Growing up in California, I was fortunate to have access to fantastic Mexican food on both sides of the border. I lived in the Mission District of San Francisco while attending university, and although my family and friends thought it was not the safest neighborhood, I would not have lived anywhere else. The streets were lined with fruit and vegetable stalls selling sacks of ripe mangoes, avocados, and chile peppers. Every corner had a take-away taco and burrito restaurant. At night the smells of cinnamon and fresh bread came wafting through my window from the nearby Mexican bakery. And half a block away was the best Mexican brunch in town.

Mexican food is one of the things I really miss living in Italy. So if the best Mexican brunch is not just around the corner, or even in your country, here is a menu to share with friends in honor of Cinco de Mayo (May 5) or Mexican Independence (September 16).

Horchata (Cinnamon Rice Water)

1 cup (200 g) long-grain white rice

2 cups (500 ml) boiling water

½ cup (100 g) sugar

About 1 teaspoon cinnamon, to taste

Ice

This is a slightly chalky, sweet rice drink that may seem usual to the unaccustomed palate, but is a brunch classic in Mexico (and fantastic for hangovers).

PLANNING AHEAD: Make the Horchata a day or two in advance. It keeps for a week in the refrigerator.

Rinse the rice. Place in a large metal or glass bowl and pour the boiling water over the rice. Let sit for 10 minutes. Drain. Cover the rice with 1 quart (1 liter) of fresh, cold water and soak for at least 2 hours, or overnight.

Strain the rice, reserving the water. Put the rice in a food processor or blender and pulverize into as fine a paste as possible. Add some of the soaking water if the mixture is too thick for the machine. Return the rice paste to the reserved soaking water. Add 2 cups (500 ml) more cold water to the mixture and stir well. Add the sugar and mix. Add cinnamon to taste.

Refrigerate for at least 2 hours. The rice will settle to the bottom. Stir well, and pour the mixture through a fine metal strainer. This will remove any large gritty sediment. Stir well before serving cold over ice.

Spicy Fruit Spears

2 ripe mangoes

2 ripe papayas

1 jicama

2 cucumbers

2 limes

Salt to taste

Mexican chile powder to taste (optional)

Peel the mangoes, papayas, jicama, and cucumbers and remove their seeds. Cut the fruit into long spear-shaped pieces. Arrange a spear or two of each type in small shallow bowls in a colorful array. Squeeze the lime juice over the top, sprinkle with salt, and a very fine dusting of spicy chile powder, if using. Finely grate some lime zest over the fruit. Serve at once.

Pico de Gallo Salsa

I large onion, finely chopped

5 tablespoons fresh lime juice

I teaspoon salt

2 fresh jalapeño chiles, seeds removed, finely chopped

2 lb (I kg) ripe tomatoes, finely chopped

½ cup (60 g) finely chopped cilantro (coriander) leaves

Salt and freshly ground black pepper to taste

PLANNING AHEAD: This salsa can be made up to 12 hours in advance. Cover and store in the refrigerator.

In a large glass bowl, marinate the onion in the lime juice and salt for 10 minutes. Add the jalapeño and marinate for 5 minutes more. Add the tomatoes and cilantro. Season with salt and pepper.

Serve with a basket of tortilla chips.

Guacamole

2 lb (I kg) ripe avocados (3–5 avocados depending on their size)

3 tablespoons fresh lime juice

¾ cup (180 ml) Pico de Gallo Salsa (see recipe above)

½ teaspoon Tabasco

Salt and freshly ground black pepper to taste

PLANNING AHEAD: Guacamole is best served soon after it is made because it tends to turn brown after a while. Cover the surface with plastic wrap to prevent discoloring if not serving immediately. A pit placed in the center of the dip can also help slow discoloration.

Peel and pit the avocados and put the pieces in a large bowl. Mash them with a fork until they are creamy and the mixture is fairly lump-free. Add the lime juice and mix well. Stir in the Pico de Gallo salsa and Tabasco. Taste for salt and pepper. Serve immediately with a basket of tortilla chips.

Pico de Gallo Salsa and **Guacamole**

Ceviche Tostadas

1 lb (500 g) very fresh red snapper or sea bass fillets, cut into 1/2-inch (1-cm) dice

1 cup (250 ml) fresh lemon juice

1 red onion, finely chopped

1 teaspoon salt

1/2 cup (125 ml) fresh lime juice

1 large stalk celery, diced

1 fresh jalapeño chile, seeds removed, finely chopped

1 fresh serrano chile, seeds removed, finely chopped

1/2 cup (100 g) finely diced red bell pepper (capsicum)

2 cups (500 g) diced ripe tomatoes, seeds removed

2 tablespoons finely chopped Italian flat-leaf parsley

1/2 cup (60 g) chopped fresh cilantro (coriander) leaves

1/4 teaspoon freshly ground black pepper

6 Tostada shells (see page 140)

1 ripe avocado

PLANNING AHEAD: The fish needs to "cook" in the lemon juice for 3 hours (or overnight). Once prepared, the ceviche lasts for 2 days in the refrigerator.

In a large glass bowl, marinate the fish and the lemon juice for at least 3 hours or overnight. The fish will turn white.

After the fish has been marinating for at least 2½ hours, begin preparing the rest of the dish.

In a separate mixing bowl, marinate the onion with the lime juice and salt for 15 minutes. Add the celery, jalapeño, serrano, and red bell pepper and let sit for 15 minutes more.

Drain the fish in a colander. Rinse with cold water. Drain well. Add the fish to the lime and onion mixture. Stir in the tomatoes, parsley, cilantro, and black pepper. Let sit for 30 minutes to allow the flavors to develop.

Just before serving, cut the avocado into ½-inch (1-cm) chunks and add to the ceviche mixture. Spoon some ceviche onto each prepared tostada shell. Serve immediately.

Huevos Rancheros

RANCHERO SAUCE

2 tablespoons extra-virgin olive oil

1 medium onion, finely chopped

1 carrot, finely chopped

Pinch of chipotle chile pepper flakes, or 1/8 teaspoon
    ground chipotle pepper

1 serrano chile, seeds removed, finely chopped

2 cloves garlic, minced

1 2/3 cups (400 g) canned tomato pulp

4 tablespoons water

Salt and freshly ground black pepper to taste

18 Corn Tortillas (see page 140)

1 recipe Frijoles de la Olla (see page 106)

12 eggs

3/4 cup (180 ml) Pico de Gallo Salsa (see page 100)

1 cup (250 ml) thinly sliced white cabbage

1/2 cup (125 ml) sour cream

PLANNING AHEAD: The ranchero sauce and the beans can be made 2 days in advance. Double the ranchero sauce recipe if making both the Huevos Rancheros and the Chile Relleños.

RANCHERO SAUCE: Heat the olive oil in a large pan over moderate heat. Add the onion, carrot, chipotle, and serrano and sauté slowly until soft. Reduce the heat if it threatens to brown. Add the garlic and cook for 1 minute. Add the tomatoes and water. Simmer for 15 minutes. Add more water if the sauce is too thick. Season with salt and pepper.

Put a warm tortilla on a serving plate. Top with some beans and ranchero sauce. Keep the plates in a warm oven while you cook the eggs.

Cook the eggs over-easy, two at a time in a skillet, with a small pad of butter. Put the eggs on top of the beans and ranchero sauce. Sprinkle the eggs with a tiny bit of salt and pepper. Return the plate to the oven until you have finished with the remaining eggs. Garnish with a spoonful of Pico de Gallo salsa and sour cream. Serve the Huevos Rancheros with some Spanish Rice, cabbage, and a basket of warm corn tortillas.

Spanish Rice

2 tablespoons extra-virgin olive oil

1 large yellow onion, finely chopped

1/8 teaspoon salt

2 cups (400 g) long-grain white rice

1/4 teaspoon cumin seeds, pounded in a mortar

3 cups (750 ml) boiling Quick Stock (see page 138)

2 ripe tomatoes, peeled, seeds removed, and flesh
    finely chopped

1/2 teaspoon good quality New Mexican red chile powder
    or Hungarian paprika

Pinch of saffron threads

Freshly ground black pepper to taste

PLANNING AHEAD: The rice can be made an hour in advance and put in a casserole dish covered with foil in a warm oven. It is also excellent when made the day before and reheated.

Heat the olive oil in a large, high-sided skillet (frying pan) over moderate heat. Add the onion and salt and sauté until soft and translucent. Add the rice and crushed cumin and stir until the rice is slightly toasted and golden. This should take about 5 minutes.

Pour in the boiling stock. The rice will pop and the mixture will come to an immediate boil. Add the tomato, chile, saffron, and some cracked black pepper. Cover. Reduce the heat to very low. Simmer, covered, for 20 minutes, or until the rice is tender.

Fluff the rice with a fork. Taste for seasoning. Transfer to a serving dish and serve hot or warm.

Jalapeño Corn Muffins

1 cup (150 g) all-purpose (plain) flour

1 cup (150 g) cornmeal

2 tablespoons sugar

1/2 teaspoon salt

1 tablespoon baking powder

1/4 teaspoon ground cumin

1/8 teaspoon cayenne

1/4 teaspoon freshly ground black pepper

1/2 cup (125 ml) finely grated parmesan

5 tablespoons extra-virgin olive oil

1 small onion, diced

1/2 cup (125 ml) diced red bell pepper (capsicum)

1 cup (250 ml) fresh or canned sweet corn kernels

1 large jalapeño chile, seeds removed, diced

3 tablespoons minced fresh cilantro (coriander)

2 large eggs, lightly beaten

3/4 cup (180 ml) whole milk

PLANNING AHEAD: The muffins will keep in an airtight container for 3–4 days. Warm before serving.

Preheat the oven to 400°F/200°C/gas 6. Butter a 12-cup muffin tray.

In a large bowl, combine the flour, cornmeal, sugar, salt, baking powder, cumin, cayenne, pepper, and parmesan. Mix well with a fork.

In a large skillet (frying pan), heat two tablespoons of olive oil over medium heat. Gently sauté the onion, red bell pepper, corn, and jalapeño until soft, but not brown. Remove from the heat. Stir in the cilantro. Cool to room temperature.

In a small bowl, combine the eggs, milk, and remaining olive oil.

Make a well in the dry mixture. Pour in the milk mixture all at once, and use a spatula to scrape all the ingredients from the pan into the well. Stir to combine. The mixture will be lumpy.

Spoon the batter into the prepared muffin cups. Bake for 20–25 minutes, or until the muffins are puffed, golden brown on top, and a toothpick inserted in the center comes out clean. Cool on a wire rack for 10 minutes. Serve warm.

Frijoles de la Olla (Beans from a Clay Pot)

1 lb (500 g) dried pinto or borlotti beans, rinsed and soaked overnight in a large bowl of water

2 bay leaves

4 cloves garlic, peeled

1 teaspoon peppercorns, coarsely crushed in a mortar

1 tiny dried red chile (peperoncino) or pinch of red pepper flakes

Salt to taste

These beans are served with the Huevos Rancheros, and are also excellent as a side dish with the Jalapeño Corn Muffins, or warm tortillas, salsa, and guacamole.

PLANNING AHEAD: The beans need to be soaked overnight. Once cooked they keep for 4–5 days in the refrigerator, and they freeze well for up to a month.

Drain the soaked beans and rinse. Put them in a large soup pot and fill with fresh water so that they are submerged by 4 inches (10 cm). Add the bay leaves, garlic, peppercorns, and chile. Bring the water to a boil over medium heat. Reduce to a simmer and cook slowly, partially covered, until the beans are tender (1 1/2–2 hours, depending upon your beans). Stir the beans occasionally to make sure they are not sticking to the bottom and add more water if needed. Taste for salt and seasoning. Serve warm.

Chile Relleños

6 large, fresh Poblano chiles with stems

4 oz (125 g) Monterey Jack cheese, cut into 6 pieces

½ cup (75 g) all-purpose (plain) flour

3 eggs, separated

⅛ teaspoon salt

Vegetable oil, for frying

1 recipe Ranchero Sauce (see page 104)

Sour cream, to garnish (optional)

PLANNING AHEAD: The chiles can be roasted and stuffed and then refrigerated overnight. Batter and fry the chiles just before serving. The Ranchero Sauce can be made a day or two in advance.

Wash and dry the chiles. Blacken them completely over an open flame. Put the charred chiles in a paper bag or in a large glass or metal bowl covered with a cloth or plastic wrap to cool. When they are cool enough to handle, gently rub the blackened skin away using your fingers and paper towels. Rinse your hands occasionally, but try to remove the burnt skin with getting the chile too wet. Keep the chile whole and intact.

Make a small lengthwise slit on one side of the chile towards the top. Use a knife to gently scrape out the seeds. Insert a piece of cheese into the chile through the slit and then close the opening firmly with a toothpick.

Pour enough vegetable oil into a large skillet (frying pan) 1 inch (2.5 cm) deep. Heat the oil over high heat until very hot, or almost smoking.

Roll the chiles in the flour to coat them. Beat the egg whites with the salt into stiff peaks. Fold the beaten whites into the broken yolks until just combined. Hold a floured chile by the stem and dip it into the egg mixture to coat completely. Drop the chile immediately into the hot oil. Cook one chile at a time. Cook, turning often, until all sides are golden brown. This should take no more than 30–60 seconds on each side. Remove with a slotted spoon and transfer to paper towels to drain. Repeat, battering and frying the chiles one at a time.

The chiles are best served immediately after frying, but they can be kept warm in the oven for 20–30 minutes. Serve the relleños with warm Ranchero Sauce and a dollop of sour cream, if desired.

Blood Orange Flan

2¾ cups (680 ml) whole milk

Zest of 1 orange, cut into wide strips

½ vanilla pod, split open

1½ cups (300 g) superfine (caster) sugar

½ cup (125 ml) blood orange juice, strained to remove pulp

3 eggs + 3 egg yolks

These flans are a nice variation from traditional crème caramel. The syrup is a ruby peach color (like a rose petal) and has a more delicate flavor than the usual caramelized sugar.

PLANNING AHEAD: The flans need to be refrigerated for 3–4 hours before serving. They can be made days in advance and refrigerated in their ramekins.

Preheat the oven to 325°F/170°C/gas 3. Set out 6 ramekins with 2-inch (5-cm) deep sides, and a roasting pan that will hold all the ramekins without touching.

Put the milk, orange zest, and vanilla pod in a heavy saucepan over medium heat. Bring to a gentle boil and then remove from the heat. Cover and let sit for 10 minutes.

Put 1 cup (200 g) of the superfine sugar in a heavy skillet (frying pan) with the orange juice. Stir over high flame until the sugar has dissolved into the juice. Stop stirring. Let the mixture bubble, shaking the pan occasionally. Cook for about 10–15 minutes, or until it is a deep ruby red, or almost brown, but not totally caramelized. Remove from the heat and swirl the pan until the bubbles have subsided. Pour some of the ruby caramel into each of the ramekins and swirl the caramel to coat the bottom and sides the ramekins. Place the ramekins in the roasting pan.

In a large bowl, whisk the eggs, egg yolks, and remaining ½ cup (100 g) of superfine sugar until pale and creamy. Strain the warm milk into a pitcher through a fine sieve to remove the orange zest and vanilla pod. Use a rubber spatula to encourage the tiny vanilla beans to pass through the sieve into the milk. Slowly pour the milk into the bowl with the egg and sugar mixture, whisking as you pour. Transfer the custard back into the milk pitcher for easy pouring into the ramekins.

Pour the custard into the prepared ramekins. Fill the roasting pan with enough hot water so it comes halfway up the sides of the ramekins. Bake for 50 minutes. The flans should be soft-set and slightly wobbly in the center, but not liquid. Remove the ramekins from the pan and cool on a wire rack. When they have cooled to room temperature, refrigerate for 3–4 hours, or overnight.

To serve: run a knife around the edge of each ramekin and invert onto serving plates.

Mexican Coffee

1 pot strong black coffee

Kahlua

Tequila

Whipped cream

Ground cinnamon (optional)

For each mug of coffee (about $^2/_3$ cup/150 ml), add 1$^1/_2$ teaspoons of Kahlua and 1 teaspoon of tequila. Add more kahlua and tequila if you like it stronger. Top with whipped cream. Sprinkle with cinnamon if desired.

Aztec Brownies

1 cup (150 g) all-purpose (plain) flour

1 teaspoon cinnamon

$^1/_4$ teaspoon cayenne pepper

$^1/_4$ teaspoon salt

$^3/_4$ teaspoon baking powder

7 oz (200 g) semisweet (dark) chocolate

3 tablespoons very strong black coffee or espresso

$^1/_2$ cup (125 g) unsalted butter, at room temperature

1 cup (200 g) sugar

2 teaspoons vanilla extract (essence)

2 eggs

These lovely gooey brownies have a hint of chile pepper.

PLANNING AHEAD: The brownies can be made 3–4 days in advance. They freeze well for up to a month.

Preheat the oven to 350°F/180°C/gas 4. Butter a 13 x 9-inch (33 x 23-cm) baking pan and line with baking paper or foil with an overhang on each side.

In a medium bowl, combine the flour, cinnamon, cayenne, salt, and baking powder. Mix well with a fork, or sift to thoroughly combine. Set aside.

Melt the chocolate with the coffee very slowly in a small pan over a larger pan of simmering water. Remove from heat and let cool to room temperature.

In a large bowl, beat the butter, sugar, and vanilla until pale and creamy. Add the eggs, one at a time, beating to just combine. Stir in the melted chocolate with a rubber spatula. Add the flour mixture in batches, stirring well between each addition.

Pour the batter into the prepared pan. Bake for 20 minutes. The brownies will look undercooked and will still be shiny in the center (a toothpick will come out sticky). Cool the brownies on a rack for 1 hour. Lift them out of the pan with the baking paper as handles. Cut into 1-inch (2.5-cm) squares. Serve.

Mediterranean Spring

Bellinis
Pecorino, Pine Nut, and Honey Crostini
Ricotta and Fava Bean Snacks
Asparagus Frittata
Leg of Lamb
Artichokes in Green Goddess Sauce
Couscous with Spiced Chickpeas
Lemon Marsala Ciambella
Espresso

Wine suggestions: Cerasuolo di Vittoria
from Valle dell'Acate or COS, or a full bodied red wine
(to accompany the lamb)

Sicily at one time or another was invaded and occupied by most of the countries in the Mediterranean. The Greeks, Arabs, Bourbons, and Spanish all left their mark on the art, architecture, language, and cuisine of the island. Sicilian cuisine has combined the influences of these various cultures to create a truly Mediterranean diet.

Lemons, oranges, and couscous came from the Arabs; chocolate, chile, and tomatoes from the Americas via the Spanish; elaborate desserts from the French; wine and olives from the Greeks. The English also played an integral role in the creation and distribution of Marsala wine.

This menu reflects what is seasonal in Sicily and the Mediterranean in the late spring. The asparagus and fennel is growing wild in the meadows, the ricotta is sweet from the spring grass, and the first cherry tomatoes are ripening in Pachino.

Bellinis

1 bottle (750 ml) prosecco or other dry sparkling wine, well chilled

1 cup (250 ml) fresh peach juice or peach nectar

Fill champagne flutes three-quarters full with wine. Add a tiny splash of fresh peach juice to each one just before serving.

Pecorino, Pine Nut, and Honey Crostini

12 thin slices North African flatbread or long, narrow loaf Italian-style bread, lightly toasted

6 oz (180 g) fresh, young pecorino cheese (or Monterey Jack if pecorino is unavailable), cut into 12 slices

2 tablespoons pine nuts

2 teaspoons good-quality honey (lavender, thyme, or rosemary honey is particularly good)

1 teaspoon fresh thyme leaves

Preheat the top grill in the oven. Put the toasted bread on a large baking sheet. Top each slice with some cheese and a few pine nuts. Put the tray under the grill and watch it closely. Grill until the cheese is melted, bubbly, and turning golden brown on top. Remove from the oven.

Use a spatula to transfer the hot crostini to a serving platter. Drizzle the honey over the crostini. Sprinkle with the thyme leaves. Serve immediately.

Ricotta and Fava Bean Snacks

3 cups (750 g) fresh fava (broad) beans, beans only, outer pods discarded

1 lb (500 g) very, fresh ewe's milk or cow's milk ricotta, drained of excess whey

2 teaspoons fresh marjoram leaves

Salt and freshly ground black pepper to taste

1 large North African flatbread, cut into small triangular pieces

Extra-virgin olive oil, to drizzle

This simple variation on crostini brings together creamy ricotta with the slightly bitter crunch of fresh fava beans.

Bring 1 quart (1 liter) of water to a boil in a medium saucepan. Salt the boiling water. Add the fava beans. Cook for 2–3 minutes, or just long enough so that the outer jacket on each bean slips away easily. Drain the beans, and run under cold water to stop them cooking. Peel the outer shells off the fava beans, reserving the bright green, split centers.

In a small bowl, mix the ricotta with the marjoram. Season with salt and pepper to taste. Spread some of the ricotta mixture on the flatbread. Put on a serving platter. Top each crostini with some of the fava beans. Drizzle some olive oil over the top, and serve.

Bellini with **Pecorino, Pine Nut, and Honey Crostini** and **Ricotta and Fava Bean Snacks**

Asparagus Frittata

1 lb (500 g) asparagus (wild asparagus is best, if available)

1 tablespoon extra-virgin olive oil

½ teaspoon salt

Pinch of chile pepper flakes, or one small, dried chile, crumbled

2 cloves garlic, minced

1 tablespoon finely chopped Italian flat-leaf parsley

1 tablespoon fresh marjoram leaves

1 tablespoon chopped fresh fennel leaves

6 eggs

2 cups (250 ml) finely grated aged pecorino cheese

Freshly ground black pepper to taste

4 leaves fresh sage, coarsely chopped

1 tablespoon unsalted butter

1 recipe Slow-Roasted Cherry Tomatoes (see page 138)

PLANNING AHEAD: The frittata can be made up to 30 minutes in advance and kept in a warm oven covered with foil.

Snap the tough, woody ends off the asparagus and discard. Rinse the stalks well and cut into 1-inch (2.5-cm) long pieces.

Use a 10-inch (25-cm) skillet (frying pan) with a flat lid. Heat the olive oil in the pan over medium heat. Add the asparagus, salt, and chile pepper and mix well. Cover and sauté, stirring occasionally, making sure the pan is not drying out and the asparagus is not browning. When the asparagus is fairly tender but still al dente, add the garlic, parsley, marjoram, and fennel. Cook for 1–2 minutes, just long enough to gently soften the garlic and herbs. Remove from the heat and let the mixture cool to room temperature.

Crack the eggs into a large bowl and beat to blend. Add the cheese and some pepper and stir. Add the cooled asparagus mixture, scraping all the goodies from the pan into the eggs with a spatula.

Use the same pan (do not clean it) that cooked the asparagus. Melt the butter in the pan over moderate heat. Add the chopped sage leaves and fry them in the butter until they are crispy but still green (not brown). Pour the egg and asparagus mixture into the pan. Use a spatula to loosen the edges of the frittata, and tilt the pan to allow the runny egg in the center to flow toward the sides. Reduce the heat if the frittata appears to be cooking too fast. Continue to cook and loosen the edges of the frittata. Shake the pan occasionally to make sure the frittata is not sticking to the bottom.

When the frittata holds together as one piece (but still has a thin layer of uncooked egg on the surface), either flip it by inverting the frittata onto the pan lid and sliding it back into the pan, or simply cover the pan with a lid and let steam finish cooking the top. Slide the frittata onto a large, flat serving plate.

Cut the frittata into triangular slices and serve with a stalk of slow roasted tomatoes.

Asparagus Frittata with Slow-Roasted Cherry Tomatoes

Leg of Lamb

2 small legs of spring lamb,
   weighing about 5–6 lb (2.5–3 kg) in total

2 teaspoons coarse sea salt

1 tablespoon black peppercorns

6 cloves garlic, peeled

1/4 cup (25 g) fresh rosemary leaves, coarsely chopped

2 tablespoons fresh oregano or marjoram leaves

6 tablespoons extra-virgin olive oil

1/2 cup (125 ml) dry white wine

1–2 cups (250–500 ml) Quick Stock (see page 138)

Extra sprigs of fresh rosemary and oregano, to garnish

This recipe calls for young, milk-fed spring lamb. Young kid is a fine substitute. It can either be roasted over hot coals on a BBQ or under a hot oven grill.

PLANNING AHEAD: Marinate the lamb overnight. Bring to room temperature before roasting the following day.

Rinse and pat the lamb dry. Remove any excess fat. Place the legs in a heavy metal roasting pan.

In a large mortar, crush the salt, pepper, and garlic into a thick paste. Add the rosemary and oregano and continue to pound to release their oils. Stir in the olive oil.

Rub the garlic and herb mixture all over the lamb. Pack the herbs into the crevices between the muscles. Make slits in the muscle if necessary to thoroughly saturate and massage every area of the meat with the herb mixture. Cover the pan with plastic wrap and refrigerate overnight (or for at least 4 hours).

Bring the lamb to room temperature before cooking. If using a BBQ, cook the legs until they are seared a deep rosy brown on the outside (but still rare inside), and transfer back to the roasting pan to finish in the oven. If using an oven grill, preheat the grill to red hot. Sear the lamb in the roasting pan under the grill, turning it to thoroughly brown all sides.

When both legs are a deep rosy brown on all sides, turn off the grill and turn the oven to bake at 400°F/200°C/gas 6 (if using the BBQ, preheat the oven while the lamb is over the coals). Pour the wine over the lamb and let it evaporate. Pour in some stock. Baste the legs occasionally, adding more stock as necessary. Cook for 25–30 minutes, or until the meat is pale pink inside. Remove from the oven. Let the lamb rest for 15 minutes.

Carve the meat onto a heated platter just before serving. Heat the pan juices, taste for seasoning, and pour through a metal strainer over the meat. Decorate the platter with sprigs of rosemary and oregano. Serve the lamb with the couscous and artichokes (see page 122).

Artichokes with Green Goddess Sauce

GREEN GODDESS SAUCE

2 cups (500 ml) plain low-fat yogurt

2 cloves garlic, crushed

1 tablespoon fresh lemon juice

1/4 cup (25 g) each, packed, of fresh basil leaves and
Italian flat-leaf parsley

2 tablespoons chopped fresh mint leaves

1 teaspoon each of fresh thyme and marjoram leaves

1 tablespoon minced chives

2 tablespoons salted capers, rinsed, soaked in water for
15 minutes, drained

1 salted anchovy, rinsed and cleaned

1 teaspoon Dijon mustard

2 tablespoons extra-virgin olive oil

Salt, freshly ground black pepper, and cayenne to taste

1 tablespoon coarse sea salt

1 lemon

12 baby artichokes

PLANNING AHEAD: The sauce lasts for 2–3 days in the refrigerator. The artichokes with the sauce can be made a day in advance. Bring to room temperature before serving.

GREEN GODDESS SAUCE: Put all the ingredients in a blender or food processor and blend until smooth. Taste for seasoning.

Bring a large pot of water to a fierce boil. Add the sea salt to the water.

Fill a large bowl with cold water and squeeze the lemon into the water. Rinse the artichokes. Peel off the tough outer leaves and peel the stems. Cut off the prickly top half of the leaves. Cut the artichokes in half vertically. Use a spoon to scoop out any fuzz in the centers. Put the cut artichoke halves in the bowl of water with the lemon (this will prevent them turning brown).

When all the artichokes are cut, transfer them from the lemon water to the boiling salt water with a slotted spoon. Boil the artichokes until tender enough to be pierced with a fork, but still al dente (about 5 minutes). Drain and rinse in cool water to stop them cooking. Drain again.

Arrange the artichokes on a serving dish with a raised rim. Pour the sauce over the artichokes. Serve with the couscous and the lamb (see below and page 120).

Couscous with Spiced Garbanzo Beans

1 1/2 cups (300 g) couscous

1 1/2 cups (375 ml) water

1/4 teaspoon salt

1/2 teaspoon each of cumin seeds, black peppercorns,
coriander seeds

1/4 teaspoon each of Hungarian paprika, turmeric, cinnamon

1/8 teaspoon ground cinnamon

1 1/2 cups (250 g) cooked garbanzo beans (chickpeas)

1 teaspoon flour

4 tablespoons extra-virgin olive oil

1/2 yellow onion, finely chopped

2 cloves garlic, minced

2 tablespoons finely chopped Italian flat-leaf parsley

PLANNING AHEAD: The spiced beans can be made in advance.

In a medium saucepan, bring the water to a boil. Add the salt. Pour in the couscous and stir. Remove the pan from the heat. Cover and let rest for 10 minutes. In a mortar, crush the cumin, peppercorns, and coriander into a fairly fine mixture. Add the paprika, turmeric, and cinnamon. Mix well.

Put the beans in a large bowl. Sprinkle the spice mixture over the top and toss to coat. Dust the spiced beans with the flour and toss again.

Heat the olive oil in a large skillet (frying pan) over moderately high heat. Add the beans and stir to coat them in the oil. Cook for 2 minutes, stirring frequently. Add the onion and cook until it is soft and beginning to brown. Add the garlic and cook for 30 seconds more. Remove the pan from the heat.

Fluff the couscous with a fork. Separate the grains and breakdown any lumps. Add the couscous to the pan with the beans. Stir well to thoroughly combine and integrate with the spices. Stir in the parsley. Transfer to a serving dish. Serve warm with the lamb.

Artichokes with Green Goddess Sauce

Lemon Marsala Ciambella

¾ cup (180 g) unsalted butter, at room temperature

2 cups (400 g) Vanilla Sugar (see page 140)

Zest of 3 large lemons, preferably organic

4 large eggs

2 cups (300 g) all-purpose (plain) flour

1 cup (150 g) cake flour

½ teaspoon salt

1 tablespoon baking powder

½ teaspoon baking soda (bicarbonate of soda)

½ cup (125 ml) whole milk

4 tablespoons fresh lemon juice

4 tablespoons dry, aged Marsala

GLAZE

⅔ cup (100 g) confectioners' (icing) sugar

1 tablespoon lemon zest

2 tablespoons fresh lemon juice

Cut strawberries and whipped cream, to garnish (optional)

A ciambella is a ring cake. To make the glaze: Combine the confectioners' sugar, lemon zest, and lemon juice to make a thick, pouring glaze.

PLANNING AHEAD: The cake lasts for 4–5 days in an airtight container.

Preheat the oven to 350°F/180°C/gas 4. Generously butter and flour a 10-inch (25-cm) kugelhopf or Bundt pan.

In a large bowl, beat the butter, sugar, and lemon zest until pale and creamy. Add the eggs one at a time until just combined. Do not overbeat.

In another large bowl, combine the flours, salt, baking powder, and baking soda and mix well. Sift one-third of the flour mixture to the butter and sugar mixture. Fold the flour into the batter with a rubber spatula as you sift. Pour in the milk and stir. Sift in another third of the flour. Continue alternating between the wet and dry ingredients until the lemon juice, Marsala, and remaining flour is all mixed into the batter. The batter should be smooth, but be careful to not overbeat as this toughens the texture of the cake.

Pour the batter into the prepared pan. Bake for 45 minutes, or until the top is a golden brown, the cake begins to pull away from the sides of the pan, and a toothpick inserted into the center comes out clean. Cool the cake on a wire rack for 10–15 minutes. Loosen the sides of the cake with a knife. Invert onto a serving plate or wire rack and carefully release from the pan. Cool until the cake is only barely warm to the touch.

Drizzle the glaze over the slightly warm cake. Allow to cool completely.

Serve slices of cake with cut strawberries and whipped cream, if desired.

Southeast Asian

I first fell in love with Southeast Asian cooking when I was a teenager living in Kuala Lumpur (Malaysia) for a semester. I was fascinated with the sprawling open food markets that sold a wide variety of vegetables, spices, live animals, and food products that seemed very exotic and pungent to my 13-year-old senses. Always an adventurous eater, I was willing to try anything short of live monkey brain. Humble street stalls with a few plastic chairs (and often questionable hygiene) sold East Indian, Chinese, and Malay dishes. I ate the most delicious vegetable roti with spicy curry wrapped in a piece of brown paper and whole chile crabs with my fingers, the likes of which I have not tasted since.

Later, in California, I was befriended by a Dutch Indonesian family and enjoyed many happy feasts in their home. Special thanks to Tina Vink and Carol and Henriette Manuputy, for numerous, unforgettable Indonesian meals, and for generously sharing their recipes for this book.

Cantaloupe Rose Cooler

1 medium cantaloupe (rock melon), weighing about
   2 lb (1 kg), seeds removed, peeled, and cut into slices

2 cups (500 g) crushed ice

2 cups (500 ml) water

1 teaspoon culinary rose water

1 tablespoon fresh lime juice

2 tablespoons sugar

Extra ice, to serve

Put all the ingredients in a blender, in the order given. Blend until smooth. Serve over ice.

Carol's Indonesian Corn Fritters

DIPPING SAUCE

1/2 cup (125 ml) sweet soy sauce

2 tablespoons fresh lime juice

1 teaspoon sambal (Indonesian red chile paste)

FRITTERS

1 carrot, peeled and grated

2 green onions (spring onions), finely chopped

2 small potatoes, peeled and grated

1 1/2 cups (275 g) fresh corn kernels (or canned)

1/4 cup (60 g) finely chopped red bell pepper (capsicum)

2 cloves garlic, crushed

1 1/2 teaspoons ground turmeric

1/4 teaspoon cayenne

2 tablespoons finely chopped fresh cilantro (coriander)

1 tablespoon finely chopped fresh basil

1/2 cup (75 g) all-purpose (plain) flour

2 eggs, lightly beaten

Corn oil, for frying

PLANNING AHEAD: The batter and dipping sauce can be made an hour or two in advance, but wait to fry the fritters until the last minute as they are best hot.

DIPPING SAUCE: Combine the ingredients in a bowl, mix well, and set aside. The dipping sauce can also be divided into tiny individual serving dishes so each guest has their own sauce.

FRITTERS: In a large bowl, combine the carrot, green onion, potato, corn, red pepper, garlic, herbs, and spices. Mix well. Sprinkle the flour over the mixture and stir to coat all the ingredients with a dusting of flour. At this point the batter can be refrigerated until it is time to fry the fritters. Just before frying, add the eggs to the batter and stir well.

Pour enough corn oil into a large, heavy skillet (frying pan) to coat the bottom 1 inch (2 cm) deep. Place the oil over high heat until it is very hot, almost smoking.

Stir the batter often between frying batches as heavier ingredients will sink to the bottom of the bowl. Drop a large spoonful (about 2 tablespoons) of batter into the hot oil. Spread the batter with a fork so that it forms a flat disk about 2 inches (5 cm) in diameter. Fry only a few fritters at a time, so that they are not touching in the pan. Turn the fritters with a slotted spoon to cook until deep golden brown on both sides. Drain on paper towel. Repeat until all the batter is cooked.

Serve the fritters hot with the dipping sauce.

Chicken Satay

2 lb (1 kg) chicken thighs, skinless, boned,
    and cut into 1-inch (2.5-cm) cubes

MARINADE

1 small onion, thinly sliced

3 cloves garlic, minced

1 fresh, spicy green chile (such as serrano), sliced horizontally,
    with seeds

1 tablespoon finely chopped, peeled fresh ginger root

4 tablespoons sweet soy sauce

2 tablespoons extra-virgin olive oil

1 stalk fresh lemongrass, cut into 1-inch (2.5-cm) pieces

2 tablespoons fresh lime juice

1 recipe Gado Gado (recipe follows)

A satay is a Southeast Asian-style kebab.

PLANNING AHEAD: The chicken is best marinated overnight.

In a medium bowl, mix together all the ingredients for the marinade. Add the chicken pieces and toss to coat. Cover and refrigerate for at least 2 hours.

Thread the marinated chicken pieces onto skewers, BBQ, cook on a cast-iron stove top grill, or under a hot oven broiler (grill) until thoroughly cooked inside and deep, crispy brown outside (about 10 minutes).

Serve the satays hot with Gado Gado dipping sauce on the side.

Gado Gado (Peanut Sauce)

2 tablespoons vegetable or olive oil

3 shallots, minced

1/2 teaspoon coriander seeds, crushed in a mortar

2 cloves garlic, minced

1/4 teaspoon sambal (Indonesian red chile paste)

1 teaspoon finely grated, peeled fresh ginger root

3/4 cup (180 ml) good-quality peanut butter

2 tablespoons sweet soy sauce

2 cups (500 ml) water

2 tablespoons fresh lime juice

Salt to taste

PLANNING AHEAD: This peanut sauce lasts for 4–5 days in the refrigerator.

Heat the oil in a large saucepan over moderate heat. Sauté the shallots and crushed coriander until the shallots are soft and translucent. Add the garlic, sambal, and ginger. Cook for 1 minute, or just long enough to soften the garlic without turning it brown. Add the peanut butter, soy sauce, and water. Stir well. Bring the mixture to a boil and reduce heat to a low simmer. Stir constantly until the sauce is the desired consistency (about 10 minutes). The sauce should be thick but pourable. Stir in the lime juice and taste for salt. Remove from the heat.

Serve at room temperature with the Chicken Satay, or as a condiment to vegetables and salads.

Chicken Satay with **Gado Gado**

Marinated Tofu Salad

7 oz (200 g) firm tofu, cut into 1/2-inch (1-cm) cubes

MARINADE

1 large clove garlic, crushed

1/4 teaspoon sambal (Indonesian red chile paste)

1 tablespoon finely grated, peeled fresh ginger root

2 tablespoons fresh lime juice

1/2 teaspoon sesame oil

1/4 cup (60 ml) soy sauce

Freshly ground black pepper to taste

SALAD

3 cups (750 g) finely sliced Chinese white cabbage

2 cups (500 g) mung bean sprouts

1 carrot, peeled and cut in julienne strips

1 cucumber, peeled, seeds removed, and cut in julienne strips

1 large, sweet red chile, or 1/2 red bell pepper (capsicum),
    seeds removed and cut in julienne strips

2 green onions (spring onions), thinly sliced;
    separate the white and green parts

2 tablespoons finely chopped Italian flat-leaf parsley

1/2 cup (60 g) fresh cilantro (coriander) leaves

4 tablespoons Gado Gado (see page 130)

1 tablespoon fresh lime juice

PLANNING AHEAD: Marinate the tofu for 2 hours (or overnight).

Whisk together all the ingredients for the marinade, and add the pieces of tofu. Marinate for at least 2 hours.

In a large salad bowl, combine the cabbage, bean sprouts, carrot, cucumber, chile, the white and pale green parts of the green onions, parsley, and cilantro. Mix well. Add the pieces of marinated tofu, reserving the marinade.

Add the lime juice and Gado Gado to the reserved marinade. Mix well. Taste for salt. Drizzle the dressing over the salad and toss. Garnish the top of the salad with the green parts of the green onions and the sesame seeds. Serve.

Green Coconut Curry with Prawns

1 tablespoon plus 1 teaspoon Thai green curry paste

1²⁄₃ cups (400 ml) coconut milk

1 long eggplant, weighing about 8 oz (250 g), cut into
    1-inch (2.5-cm) cubes

8 oz (250 g) green beans, stems trimmed and long ones
    snapped in half

1 red bell pepper (capsicum), sliced into thin 2-inch (5-cm)
    long strips

1 zucchini (courgette), cut in half lengthwise and then sliced
    into half-moon pieces

1 yellow crookneck squash, cut into half-moon pieces

½ cup (125 g) thinly sliced bamboo shoots

10–12 fresh basil leaves, torn

1 teaspoon Thai fish sauce

1 lb (500 g) medium-large whole uncooked prawns

¼–½ cup (60–125 ml) vegetable stock or water

Few sprigs of Vietnamese mint, to garnish

1 lime, cut into wedges, to garnish

PLANNING AHEAD: The curry can be made in advance, but remove from the heat when the vegetables are still more al dente than you would serve them, so they do not become mushy when reheated.

Place the green curry paste and half the coconut milk in a large skillet (frying pan) over moderate heat until very fragrant and bubbly. Add the eggplant, toss in the sauce, and cook for 3 minutes. Add the green beans and bell pepper. Stir, then cover and cook for 5–7 minutes. Add the zucchini, squash, bamboo shoots, the remaining coconut milk, and fish sauce. When the vegetables are tender, but still al dente, add the prawns and basil. Add some vegetable stock or water if the curry gets too dry. Cook until the prawns are opaque/pink. Taste for salt and seasoning. Remove from the heat.

Serve the curry hot with steamed Thai jasmine rice. Garnish with the mint and wedges of lime.

Green Coconut Curry with Prawns

Henriette's Coconut Torte with Mangoes

1 loaf white bread, weighing 12 oz (350 g), crusts removed

2 cups (500 ml) whole milk

Finely grated zest of 2 limes

Two 15.5 oz (440 g) cans young coconut meat in syrup, drained, and grated or pulsed in food processor

¾ cup (150 g) sugar

1 tablespoon vanilla extract (essence)

½ teaspoon salt

4 tablespoons unsalted butter, melted

1 egg, lightly beaten

2 ripe mangoes

2 tablespoons fresh lime juice

Shredded lime zest, to garnish

PLANNING AHEAD: The bread needs to soak in the milk for 20 minutes. The cake keeps for 3–4 days in an airtight container.

In a large bowl, crumble and tear the bread into small pieces. Pour the milk over the top and let sit for 20 minutes.

Preheat the oven to 350°F/180°C/gas 4. Butter and flour a 9 x 2-inch (23 x 5-cm) round cake pan.

Use a fork to smash the bread and break up any big lumps. The mixture should look mushy, like thick batter. Add the lime zest, coconut meat, sugar, vanilla, salt, and butter and mix well. Stir in the egg. Pour the batter into the prepared pan.

Bake for 65–75 minutes, or until the cake is golden brown on top and a toothpick comes out clean. Cool in the pan on a rack for 10 minutes. Loosen the edges with a knife. Invert the cake onto a cooling rack and let cool completely.

When ready to serve the cake, prepare the mangoes. Cut the fleshy lobes off both sides of the mango pit. Cut a grid pattern, almost to the peel, on the cut-side of the mango halves. Flip the mango peel upward, exposing the cut cubes of mango like porcupine quills. Cut the cubes of mango away from the peel. Toss the mango cubes in a bowl with the lime juice. Serve some mango with the slices of coconut torte. Garnish with the shredded lime zest.

Basics

Quick Stock

1 large onion, peeled, cut in half

1 celery stalk with leaves plus leafy top of another stalk, cut in half

1 large carrot, peeled, cut in half

2 large cloves garlic, peeled

1 large bay leaf

1 small dried chile pepper, whole

3 cardamom pods, whole

2 teaspoons black peppercorns, whole

1 teaspoon coarse sea salt

Handful of fresh Italian parsley with stems, rinsed

1 tablespoon fresh thyme

1 small potato, peeled (optional)

PLANNING AHEAD: The stock freezes well for months and lasts for about four days in the refrigerator.

Homemade stock makes a huge difference in the flavor of any dish. This recipe uses a pressure cooker, so the whole process is quick and easy. Depending upon whether you want chicken, squab, or beef stock, use: half a small chicken (preferably free-range), or 1 squab (pigeon), or 10 oz (300 g) beef muscle and a good beef shank "soup" bone.

Put all ingredients into a 3½-quart (3.5-liter) pressure cooker, add water up to the indicated line (about 2½ quarts/2.5 liters). Lock the lid. Place over medium to medium-high heat until the pressure vent begins to blow steam. This will occur after 10–15 minutes, or up to 25 minutes if using frozen meat and bones. Turn heat down to low. Cook for another 45 minutes to 1 hour. Remove from the heat. Let stand for 5–10 minutes, then release the lid.

Put a colander over a large bowl or pot. Drain the contents of the pressure cooker through the colander to separate the pieces of meat and vegetable from the stock. Reserve the pieces of meat, either for *bollito* (boiled beef) sandwiches or the chicken and squab for pâté. Discard the used vegetables and bones. Allow the stock to cool slightly, then cover and refrigerate until ready to use. Skim off any congealed fat on the surface of the stock before using.

Slow-Roasted Cherry Tomatoes

2 lb (1 kg) ripe cherry tomatoes, in clusters on their vines

4 tablespoons extra-virgin olive oil

Salt to taste

PLANNING AHEAD: Prepare the tomatoes the night before your brunch. They last for 5–6 days in an airtight container in the refrigerator.

Preheat the oven to 400°F/200°C/gas 6. Oil a large baking sheet. Put the clusters of cherry tomatoes still on their vines on the baking sheet. Drizzle the oil over the tomatoes and sprinkle with salt.

Put the tray of tomatoes in the hot oven and immediately reduce the oven temperature to 350°F/180°C/gas 4. Bake for 15 minutes. Reduce the heat to 300°F/150°C/gas 4 and bake for 15 minutes more. Continue reduce the oven temperature in even intervals every 10–15 minutes until the oven is at its lowest temperature. Turn the oven off. Leave the tomatoes in the closed oven to cool overnight. The next morning they are ready to eat.

Polenta (creamy or baked)

1½ cups (250 g) polenta (stone-ground cornmeal)

1½ quarts (1.5 liters) boiling water

1 teaspoon salt

2 tablespoons butter

½ cup (60 g) finely grated parmesan cheese

Freshly ground black pepper to taste

Creamy polenta has to be eaten the day it is made. Baked polenta is made from yesterday's polenta.

Use a large 6-quart (6-liter) pot and a large metal bowl that fits on top of the pot. Fill the bottom quarter of the pot with water, making sure the bottom of the bowl does not touch the water. Fill another medium saucepan or a kettle with 1½ quarts (1.5 liters) of water. Bring both sets of water to a boil. Pour the 1½ quarts (1.5 liters) of boiling water and salt into the metal bowl. Stir the water to create a whirlpool. Gradually pour in the polenta until smooth. Stir the polenta for 1–2 minutes. Cover with foil. Reduce to a low simmer. Cook for 1½ hours. Stir every 30 minutes to make sure the polenta is not sticking. Be sure to reseal the foil after stirring.

After 1½ hours the polenta will be thick and creamy with no raw taste. Stir in the butter, parmesan, and black pepper. Taste for salt.

For baked polenta: Put the warm polenta into a 9 x 5-inch (23 x 13-cm) loaf pan and smooth the top with a spatula. Cool, cover, and refrigerate at least 3 hours. Unmold the polenta onto a wooden cutting board. Cut into ½-inch (1-cm) thick slices and cut each slice in half to form rectangular pieces. Place the slices on an oiled baking sheet. Sprinkle with more Parmesan and herbs and put under a hot broiler (grill). When the tops are golden, turn the slices over and brown the other side. Keep warm until ready to serve.

Herb Cream Cheese

1 cup (250 g) plain cream cheese, at room temperature

1 clove garlic, crushed

1 tablespoon dry vermouth

1 green onion (spring onion), finely chopped

1 tablespoon finely chopped fresh chives

1 teaspoon each of fresh thyme, finely chopped Italian parsley, and marjoram or oregano

¼ teaspoon freshly ground black pepper

PLANNING AHEAD: Keeps for 2–3 days in the refrigerator.

Stir all the ingredients together and let the flavors develop for 30 minutes.

Croutons

3 cups (200 g) cubed day-old bread

3 tablespoons extra-virgin olive oil

2 cloves garlic, crushed

¼ teaspoon salt

½ teaspoon thyme

½ teaspoon marjoram

3 tablespoons finely grated parmesan cheese

Preheat the oven to 400°F/200°C/gas 6. Put the bread cubes in a large bowl. In a small bowl, stir the oil, garlic, salt, thyme, and marjoram. Pour the oil mixture over the bread and toss well. Sprinkle the cheese over the bread and stir. Put the seasoned bread cubes on a large baking sheet. Bake for 10–15 minutes, or until golden brown. Turn the bread cubes over with a spatula half way through the baking to ensure all sides are evenly toasted. Remove from the oven and let cool.

Sweet Roll Dough

I cube (25 g) compressed fresh yeast
    or 2 tablespoons active dry yeast
I cup (250 ml) warm whole milk
3 cups (450 g) all-purpose (plain) flour
3 tablespoons sugar
I egg, lightly beaten
I teaspoon salt
4 tablespoons unsalted butter, at room temperature

Dissolve the yeast in the warm milk in a small glass or plastic bowl. Add a pinch of flour and sugar to the milk and yeast mixture and let stand for 3–5 minutes, until the milk is foamy. Put the flour and sugar in a large mixing bowl. Pour in the milk and yeast mixture. Mix with a bread hook on medium-low speed until combined and sticky, about 2 minutes. Add the egg and salt and continue mixing. When the egg is incorporated into the dough, add the butter 1 tablespoon at a time. Beat for 2–3 minutes more, or until the dough is soft, elastic, and quite sticky.

Rinse a large glass or plastic bowl in hot water and do not dry the bowl. Put the dough in the bowl, cover with plastic wrap and a clean kitchen towel, and put aside in a warm place to rise for 45 minutes to 1 hour. The dough will double in bulk.

Corn Tortillas and Tostada Shells

2 cups (300 g) masa harina
1½ cups (325 ml) warm water

These are Mexican tortillas, not the Spanish version which is more like a frittata. Homemade corn tortillas are simple to make and much tastier than store-bought tortillas.

Put the masa harina in a large bowl. Add enough warm water to make a soft, workable dough. Work the dough through your fingers until it is smooth, consistent, and can easily be formed into a ball. Add more water if the dough is too crumbly, or later becomes too dry during the rolling out process. Pinch off a small quantity of dough (about 1 tablespoon) and roll it into a ball. Flatten the dough between two pieces of waxed paper with a rolling pin. Roll into a 5-inch (13-cm) circle that is ¹⁄₁₆-inch (2-mm) thick.

To make tostada shells, fry the corn tortillas one at a time in a small amount (2–4 tablespoons) of vegetable oil until they are golden and crisp. Drain on paper towels. Serve warm.

Vanilla Sugar

2 lb (I kg) granulated sugar
I vanilla pod

Split a vanilla bean lengthwise and scrape the seeds into the sugar. Rub the pod with sugar between your fingers to release all the seeds and leave the scraped out pod in the sugar.

Whole-Wheat Pastry

1 cup (150 g) unbleached white flour
½ cup (75 g) whole-wheat (wholemeal) flour
⅛ teaspoon salt
½ cup (125 g) cold unsalted butter
2–3 tablespoons ice water

Combine the two flours and salt in a large bowl. Cut in the butter with a pastry cutter or your fingers until the mixture resembles coarse bread crumbs. Add 2 tablespoons of water and work quickly with your fingers to integrate the dough. Form into a disk. If the dough is too dry to hold together, add the third tablespoon of water. Wrap in plastic wrap and refrigerate for 30 minutes to 1 hour.

Sweet Egg Pastry

1 cup (150 g) all-purpose (plain) flour
¼ cup (50 g) sugar
Pinch of salt
½ cup (125 g) cold unsalted butter, cut into chunks
1 egg yolk

Combine the flour, sugar, and salt in a large bowl. Cut in the butter with a pastry cutter or use your fingers until the mixture resembles coarse bread crumbs. Add the egg yolks. Mix quickly with your fingers. Press the dough into a disk shape. Wrap in waxed paper and refrigerate for 1 hour.

Shortcrust Pastry

1⅓ cups (180 g) all-purpose (plain) flour
¼ teaspoon salt
½ cup (125 g) cold unsalted butter, cut into pieces
2½ tablespoons ice water

Mix the flour and salt in a large bowl. Cut the butter into the flour with a pastry cutter or rub between your fingers until the butter is the size of peas. Add 2 to 2½ tablespoons of ice water, only enough for the dough to barely hold together. Form the dough into a round disk, wrap in plastic and refrigerate for 1 hour to 2 days.

Use a 9-inch (23-cm) springform pan or removable bottom tart pan with 2 inch (5 cm) sides. Roll the dough out on a floured surface into a 15-inch (37-cm) round. Line the pan with the dough, crimping the edges in a decorative fashion. Refrigerate for 30 more minutes.

Preheat the oven to 400°F/200°C/gas 6. Line the pastry with waxed paper or foil and fill with dried beans or pie weights. Bake blind for 15 minutes. Gently remove the foil and weights, prick the pastry with a fork, and bake for 15 more minutes, or until golden. Cool on a rack.

Index